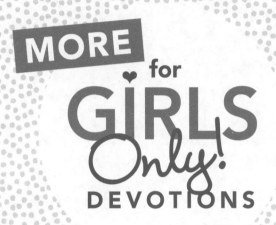

MORE for
GiRLS
Only!
DEVOTIONS

MORE
for
GIRLS
Only!
DEVOTIONS

written by **CAROLYN LARSEN** ✳ illustrated by **COLONEL MOUTARDE**

Tyndale House Publishers, Inc.
Carol Stream, Illinois

Visit www.cool2read.com.

Visit Carolyn Larsen online at www.carolynlarsen.com.

TYNDALE and Tyndale's quill logo are registered trademarks of Tyndale House Publishers, Inc.

More for Girls Only! Devotions

Designed by Jennifer Phelps

Edited by Sarah Rubio

Scripture quotations are taken from the *Holy Bible*, New Living Translation, copyright © 1996, 2004, 2015 by Tyndale House Foundation. Used by permission of Tyndale House Publishers, Inc., Carol Stream, Illinois 60188. All rights reserved.

For manufacturing information regarding this product, please call 1-800-323-9400.

ISBN 978-1-4964-0196-0

Printed in the United States of America

21 20 19 18 17 16 15
7   6   5   4   3   2   1

Contents

Stayin' Strong

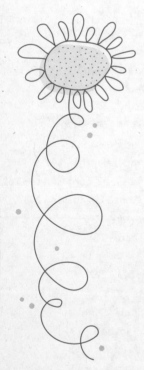

A final word: Be strong in the Lord and in his mighty power.
EPHESIANS 6:10

NATALIE PRETTY MUCH knows right from wrong. After all, some things are no-brainers. Like cheating on an exam—that's wrong. Plain and simple. But . . . Natalie and science do not get along. She studies and studies, but the information just doesn't stick in her brain. Natalie's grade keeps slipping lower and lower, and she is getting more and more frustrated. Now her parents are on her case too. So when a friend tells her about a sneaky way to cheat on the next science exam, Natalie actually thinks about it. After all, she really *needs* a good grade!

Natalie knows cheating is wrong . . . for any reason. But now she is feeling tempted. What should she do?

Have you ever been tempted to cheat or do something else that you knew was wrong? Did you feel like you had a really good reason for doing the wrong thing? Was it hard for you to fight off the temptation and stay true to what you know is right?

Ephesians 6:10 reminds you that God is your strength. You can ask for his help in fighting the temptation to do wrong. God is steady and constant—he never changes. He will always be with you, and he is stronger than any temptation you might face. So get closer to God to get the strength you need. Ask him to help you. God knows that temptation can be tough and you will need his strength and power to resist it. Maybe that's one reason why the verse says "a final word"—it's the bottom line, the foundation of how to fight temptation. Be strong in God's strength and power.

CHECKUP TIME

On a scale of 1 to 5, how do you handle the temptation to cheat?

1 = never
2 = not very often
3 = sometimes
4 = most of the time
5 = always

I fight temptation as hard as I can.

1   2   3   4   5

I believe God will help me in tough situations.

1   2   3   4   5

I believe some things, like cheating, are always wrong, no matter what.

1   2   3   4   5

When tempted, I pray right away and ask God to help me be strong.

1   2   3   4   5

I am willing to accept that doing what is right is better than being the best.

1   2   3   4   5

KEY

MOSTLY 1s You are in big trouble. Promise yourself to pray for God's help next time you are tempted. See what happens.

MOSTLY 2s You aren't taking sin very seriously. Take a good look at today's Scriptures to align yourself with what God thinks.

MOSTLY 3s Middle of the road—not terrible and not great. You can do better!

MOSTLY 4s You're on the right track. Keep depending on God's strength.

MOSTLY 5s Congratulations! You're calling on God's strength and power to help you fight off temptation.

THINGS TO DO

○ Make a list of times in the Bible where you see God's power and strength at work.

○ Write down the times God's strength and power have helped you.

○ Memorize Ephesians 6:10.

○ Use the index at the back of your Bible or a commentary to find a few more verses about God's strength and power.

THINGS TO REMEMBER

Do not deceive or cheat one another.
LEVITICUS 19:11

God arms me with strength,
and he makes my way perfect.
PSALM 18:32

[The Lord] renews my strength.
He guides me along right paths,
bringing honor to his name.
PSALM 23:3

If you are faithful in little things, you will be faithful in large ones. But if you are dishonest in little things, you won't be honest with greater responsibilities. **LUKE 16:10**

Cling to your faith in Christ, and keep your conscience clear. For some people have deliberately violated their consciences; as a result, their faith has been shipwrecked.
1 TIMOTHY 1:19

It is a great deal better to live a holy life than to talk about it. Lighthouses do not ring bells and fire cannons to call attention to their shining—they just shine.
D. L. MOODY

Nothing speaks louder or more powerfully than a life of integrity.
CHARLES SWINDOLL

I would prefer even to fail with honor than to win by cheating.
SOPHOCLES

Don't Go It Alone

Two people are better off than one, for they can help each other succeed.

ECCLESIASTES 4:9

SAMMIE COULDN'T GET THE BABIES out of her mind. She had watched a news report on TV about babies who were born with HIV. They were sick. They were sad. They cried a lot. They really needed to be held and hugged. But the nurses and hospital workers just didn't have time to sit and hold the babies all the time. They had other work to do. "I wish I could just go to every hospital and hold every single baby!" Sammie told her mom.

She was still thinking about the babies the next day when she suddenly got an idea. *What if I make some super soft blankets and give them to hospitals? The nurses can wrap the babies up tight in the blankets. Maybe that will feel like hugs for the babies.*

Sammie used her own money to buy as much material as she could. She cut fabric and tied pieces together to make blankets. But before long she was discouraged. "I've used all the fabric I bought and I'm out of money. Besides, I can only make, like, two blankets a day," she told her friend Jill. "At this rate it will take years to make enough blankets for all the babies."

"Well, I could help you," Jill said. "We could ask people to donate money for fabric and I could help you make blankets."

"Really? Do you want to do that?" Sammie asked.

"Yes. I was kind of hoping you would ask me to help," Jill said.

Together they raised money from their neighbors and church friends and worked to make blankets. They could make twice as many blankets together as Sammie could alone. It was great!

Sammie experienced the truth of Ecclesiastes 4:9. You can get a whole lot more done if you have partners. God planned for people to help each other as much as possible. Why? Because it's good to share the work, share the joy, and even share the hard times. It's always better to know you aren't alone. Look around and see who can help you with something you need to do—maybe you'll see people you can help too!

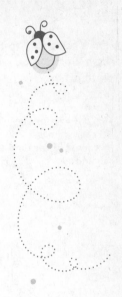

CHECKUP TIME

On a scale of 1 to 5, how well do you work with others?

1 = never
2 = not very often
3 = sometimes
4 = most of the time
5 = always

I ask others how they would do things.

1   2   3   4   5

I work hard to help other people with their projects.

1   2   3   4   5

I try to find friends to help me when I have a big task.

1   2   3   4   5

I share my problems and my joys with a special friend.

1   2   3   4   5

I think I work better with a team than alone.

1   2   3   4   5

KEY

MOSTLY 1s Don't be a lone wolf! You need to work on cooperating with others and allowing others to help you.

MOSTLY 2s You are a bit too self-focused. Look around and see who might help you or whom you could help.

MOSTLY 3s You know the value of teamwork, but you don't always put that knowledge to good use.

MOSTLY 4s Not bad! You understand that teamwork yields good results.

MOSTLY 5s Yay for you! You get it! God wants us to help one another.

THINGS TO DO

- ◯ Find a story in the Bible where people worked together to get a job done.

- ◯ Make a list of projects you could use help with.

- ◯ Look around—can you see ways you could help others?

- ◯ Memorize Ecclesiastes 4:9.

THINGS TO REMEMBER

If one person falls, the other can reach out and help. But someone who falls alone is in real trouble.
ECCLESIASTES 4:10

Don't look out only for your own interests, but take an interest in others, too.
PHILIPPIANS 2:4

In his grace, God has given us different gifts for doing certain things well. **ROMANS 12:6**

All of you together are Christ's body, and each of you is a part of it. **1 CORINTHIANS 12:27**

Share each other's burdens, and in this way obey the law of Christ. **GALATIANS 6:2**

Coming together is a beginning; keeping together is progress; working together is success.
HENRY FORD

Alone we can do so little; together we can do so much.
HELEN KELLER

Individually, we are one drop. Together, we are an ocean.
RYUNOSUKE SATORO

God Is Not Impressed

Don't be selfish; don't try to impress others. Be humble, thinking of others as better than yourselves.

PHILIPPIANS 2:3

"I GET ALL THE SOLOS IN CHOIR," Kylie bragged. "Everyone thinks that my voice is Broadway quality. You know the end-of-school choir concert is coming up. I'm sure I'll get the big solo."

Maria and Shauna just looked at each other and sighed.

"Well, maybe someone else will get the big solo this time," Maria said.

"Oh come on. Who else would get it?" Kylie snapped.

"Well . . . maybe Shauna will. She has a pretty voice," Maria said.

"Ha! Yeah, right. Like Shauna could sing *my* solo! She doesn't have my range. This is an important concert. Mrs. Davis wouldn't give the solo to someone else. You're hilarious, Maria. Singing is my thing. It's what God made me to do. I'm the best singer in the whole school."

Kylie was so busy letting everyone know how awesome she was that she didn't care how she made other people feel. She didn't even notice when Shauna left the room. But Maria noticed. She felt bad for Shauna . . . and for Kylie, who couldn't see that she was hurting her friends, not impressing them.

Kylie has a problem. She cares more

about her reputation as the greatest singer in the school than she cares about her friends' feelings. That's not right. If Kylie would learn from Philippians 2:3, she wouldn't spend so much energy trying to impress others. She might even be able to compliment Shauna's singing.

God wants his followers to think more about encouraging others than bragging to impress them. We should care about others and encourage them to be the best they can be. Maybe you don't think you're as bad as Kylie, but be honest— do you spend more time thinking about how you can impress people or how you can encourage them? Look around for someone you can encourage today!

CHECKUP TIME

On a scale of 1 to 5, how important is it to you to impress others?

1 = never
2 = not very often
3 = sometimes
4 = most of the time
5 = always

I mention how well my friends do things—even things I know that I'm good at.

1   2   3   4   5

It's not important to me that my friends know how great I am at doing things.

1   2   3   4   5

I don't always have to be the best.

1   2   3   4   5

My friends are more important to me than impressing others.

1   2   3   4   5

I know when to back off so my friends can shine.

1   2   3   4   5

KEY

MOSTLY 1s Whoa! There are some ego issues here. You need to work on your care for others—and your own humility. Ask God to give you a healthy view of yourself.

MOSTLY 2s You could certainly stand to work on being a better friend and less focused on yourself. Pray for opportunities to encourage others.

MOSTLY 3s So-so. You still have some work to do with encouraging others. Don't give up!

MOSTLY 4s You do care about others, but maybe you still need some humility lessons. Keep practicing Philippians 2:3.

MOSTLY 5s Yay! You have your ego under control, and you are a caring friend. Keep up the good work!

THINGS TO DO

○ Pay some attention to your friends. Give one compliment to someone each day . . . and mean it.

○ Ask a friend to hold you accountable by giving you a nudge or another signal when you start bragging.

○ Memorize Philippians 2:3.

○ Ask God to help you remember that all your talents are gifts from him.

THINGS TO REMEMBER

God opposes the proud but gives grace to the humble. **JAMES 4:6**

Watch out! Don't do your good deeds publicly, to be admired by others, for you will lose the reward from your Father in heaven.
MATTHEW 6:1

You rescue the humble,
but you humiliate the proud.
PSALM 18:27

Let us think of ways to motivate one another to acts of love and good works. **HEBREWS 10:24**

Humility does not mean thinking less of yourself than of other people, nor does it mean having a low opinion of your own gifts. It means freedom from thinking about yourself one way or the other at all.
WILLIAM TEMPLE

Swallow your pride occasionally, it's not fattening.
FRANK TYGER

A proud man is always looking down on things and people: and, of course, as long as you are looking down, you cannot see something that is above you.
C. S. LEWIS

No Worries

Can all your worries add a single moment to your life?
MATTHEW 6:27

MOLLY'S NICKNAME is the Queen of What-If. That's because her constant question is, "What if . . . ?" She has a habit of always looking on the dark side of things. Grandma says Molly's glass is always half empty, never half full . . . whatever that means. For example, if her parents announce, "We're going to the beach tomorrow!" Molly's response is, "What if it rains?" "What if the car doesn't start?" "What if we get sunburned?" and a million other what-ifs.

No matter what's happening, Molly can find something to worry about. She has a way of putting a dark cloud over pretty much everything, even really good and fun things, like going to a party or shopping at her favorite store or eating at her favorite restaurant or visiting much-missed cousins. Instead of looking forward to things with excitement and joy, Molly worries that she'll trip or do something else embarrassing at the party, that she won't find any clothes she likes in her size, that she'll get food poisoning, or that her favorite cousin will have changed and won't want to hang out with her anymore. The things Molly worries about usually don't come true, but she just can't stop obsessing over worst-case scenarios.

What Molly needs to remember is that all her worry will not change the way things turn out one bit. Worry is not some magic way to make things turn out well. Worry can't make you happier. Worry can't make you—or anyone else—live longer. Worry won't make you richer or prettier or stronger or smarter. Worry doesn't do anything good. In fact, worry robs you of the chance to be happy. It keeps you from enjoying what's going on right now.

Could you also be called a Queen of What-If? The worst thing worry does is keep you from trusting God and actually noticing the wonderful things he does for you. When you feel worry creeping into your thoughts, ask God to help you push it away and to remind you of his love and care for you. No worries . . . only trust!

CHECKUP TIME

On a scale of 1 to 5, how well do you handle worry?

1 = never
2 = not very often
3 = sometimes
4 = most of the time
5 = always

When I get worried or scared, my first course of action is to pray.

1   2   3   4   5

I look on the bright side of things instead of worrying about what bad things could happen.

1   2   3   4   5

I believe God is in control.

1   2   3   4   5

When worry starts, I ask someone I trust to pray with me about it.

1   2   3   4   5

I can see the adventure in new experiences without worrying about how things might turn out.

1   2   3   4   5

KEY

MOSTLY 1s Worry has a hold on you! Using a concordance or a Bible website, look up some Bible verses about trusting God.

MOSTLY 2s Could be worse, but you still need to work on things. Ask God to help you remember to trust him when you feel tempted to worry.

MOSTLY 3s Middle of the road—sometimes you worry and sometimes you don't. Try to think of one situation every day where you see God taking care of things.

MOSTLY 4s Pretty good. Keep working on trusting God and seeing the good even in difficult situations.

MOSTLY 5s Congratulations! You are *not* a Queen of What-If!

THINGS TO DO

○ Write down what you're worrying about. What's the worst thing that could happen? How likely is it that this thing will happen? Even if it did happen, would God still love you? Would he still have a good plan for your life? Would he help you get through it?

○ Take one thing you're worried about, and each time worry pops into your mind, stop and pray about it.

○ Memorize a verse about trusting God.

○ Ask someone you trust to pray with you and for you about your worries.

THINGS TO REMEMBER

Trust in the LORD with all your heart; do not depend on your own understanding. **PROVERBS 3:5**

The seed that fell among the thorns represents those who hear God's word, but all too quickly the message is crowded out by the worries of this life and the lure of wealth, so no fruit is produced. **MATTHEW 13:22**

This is my command—be strong and courageous! Do not be afraid or discouraged. For the LORD your God is with you wherever you go. **JOSHUA 1:9**

Don't worry about anything; instead, pray about everything. Tell God what you need, and thank him for all he has done. **PHILIPPIANS 4:6**

You will keep in perfect peace
all who trust in you,
all whose thoughts are fixed on you!
ISAIAH 26:3

Worrying is like a rocking chair, it gives you something to do, but it gets you nowhere.
GLENN TURNER

Any concern too small to be turned into a prayer is too small to be made into a burden.
CORRIE TEN BOOM

Faith is putting all your eggs in God's basket, then counting your blessings before they hatch.
RAMONA C. CARROLL

Listen Up!

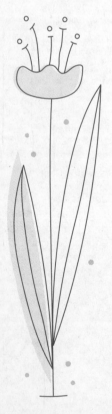

Fools think their own way is right, but the wise listen to others.

PROVERBS 12:15

"KATIE, DON'T YOU HAVE a book report due at the end of the month? It's a big book, isn't it? Maybe you should start reading it," Mom suggested.

"Ugh, it looks so boring," Katie moaned. "I'll start it later."

"It would be a good idea to make a chart of how many pages you need to read each day in order to finish the book and have enough time left to write the report. I can help you with that," Mom said gently.

"Mom! I'll get the report done in plenty of time," Katie snapped back.

But she didn't start reading the next day, or even the next week.

A week later Mom said again, "Katie, you're running out of time to get your book read and the report written. You only have about two and a half weeks now." Katie stomped up the stairs to her room, slammed the door, and plopped down on her bed with the big, boring-looking book. In about two minutes she was sound asleep.

Several days later Mom said, "I'm not going to mention it again, Katie. You know your book report is due in just over a week. I've advised you to get busy on it. I even offered to help you make up a schedule. You've ignored all my advice and offers of help, so . . . now you'll just have to live with the results."

About two days before the book report was due, Katie panicked. "I don't have time to read the book. What am I going to do? I'll get a bad grade. Mom, help!"

But it was too late for Katie. She didn't listen to good advice when Mom offered it. Now she would have to live with the consequences.

Does this sound familiar? Do you get annoyed when your parents, teachers, or other adults try to give you advice? The Bible says that only fools think they always know best (read Proverbs 12:15 again). It's foolish to ignore good advice from people who are older than you, know more than you, and love you.

CHECKUP TIME

On a scale of 1 to 5, how good are you at taking advice?

1 = never
2 = not very often
3 = sometimes
4 = most of the time
5 = always

I listen to suggestions from my parents.

1   2   3   4   5

I try to talk to older, trustworthy people who have a good perspective on things and give good advice.

1   2   3   4   5

I don't insist on doing things my way.

1   2   3   4   5

I know I can learn from the advice of others.

1   2   3   4   5

I follow the advice found in the Bible.

1   2   3   4   5

KEY

MOSTLY 1s Whoa! An advice follower you are not! Better work on that. Ask God to help you benefit from the wisdom of others.

MOSTLY 2s A little better, but you still have a lot of work to do.

MOSTLY 3s Medium. Maybe you don't take advice because you have trouble trusting people? Ask God to bring some trustworthy advisers into your life (or to recognize the ones he's already brought you).

MOSTLY 4s You usually follow advice and probably learn a lot from it.

MOSTLY 5s Congratulations! You trust God and the people he's put in your life, so you benefit from wise advice!

THINGS TO DO

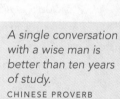

○ Take one piece of trustworthy advice in the next couple of days and see how things turn out for you.

○ Memorize Proverbs 12:15.

○ Pray about your attitude. Ask God to make you willing to listen to others.

○ Make a list of people you trust and respect—people whose advice you would listen to.

THINGS TO REMEMBER

To one person the Spirit gives the ability to give wise advice; to another the same Spirit gives a message of special knowledge. **1 CORINTHIANS 12:8**

Oh, the joys of those who do not follow the advice of the wicked, or stand around with sinners, or join in with mockers. **PSALM 1:1**

The LORD says, "I will guide you along the best pathway for your life. I will advise you and watch over you." **PSALM 32:8**

If you need wisdom, ask our generous God, and he will give it to you. He will not rebuke you for asking. **JAMES 1:5**

Don't let anyone think less of you because you are young. Be an example to all believers in what you say, in the way you live, in your love, your faith, and your purity. **1 TIMOTHY 4:12**

A single conversation with a wise man is better than ten years of study.
CHINESE PROVERB

One friend, one person who is truly understanding, who takes the trouble to listen to us as we consider a problem, can change our whole outlook on the world.
DR. E. H. MAYO

Big egos have little ears.
ROBERT SCHULLER

Inside-Out Beauty

Don't be concerned about the outward beauty of fancy hairstyles, expensive jewelry, or beautiful clothes. You should clothe yourselves instead with the beauty that comes from within, the unfading beauty of a gentle and quiet spirit, which is so precious to God.
1 PETER 3:3-4

MAYA WAS POUTING . . . again. "Why can't I have those jeans? All my friends have them. Everyone has them. I look like a loser because I have plain old jeans," she moaned. Her mom sighed and went into the kitchen. Maya followed her. "Come on, Mom. I just want to look cool like everyone else."

"Maya, we've been through this before. Today it's jeans that cost over a hundred dollars a pair. Last week it was shoes that were just as expensive. Before that it was getting your hair cut at a certain salon and getting second ear piercings. It's too much." Mom sighed again.

Maya quietly said, "I just want to be pretty, like the popular girls. That's all."

Mom sat down and took Maya's hands in hers. "Sweetheart, jeans and haircuts and jewelry have nothing to do with real beauty. Sure, those things can make you *feel* pretty for a little bit, but that feeling wears off pretty fast."

"What do you mean?" Maya asked.

"Well, just because a person has stylish clothes doesn't mean she is kind. It doesn't mean she is generous or helpful. It doesn't mean she cares about others. Think about it. The people you think are really beautiful—the people you really want to be like—are people whose beauty comes from inside, from their hearts. Real beauty comes from God's love shining through you to others."

Do you ever catch yourself focusing more on what is in your closet than what is in your heart? The "stuff" that you like to wear can make you feel pretty . . . and that's okay. But it isn't what gives you real beauty. Just as 1 Peter 3:3-4 says, real beauty comes from the inside— from God's love shin- ing through you.

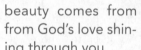

On a scale of 1 to 5, what is your attitude about beauty?

1 = never
2 = not very often
3 = sometimes
4 = most of the time
5 = always

I am happy even when I wear "nothing special" kind of clothes.

    1   2   3   4   5

I don't care about anyone else's opinion of my style.

    1   2   3   4   5

I care more about kindness than designer clothes.

    1   2   3   4   5

I want people to see God's love in me more than to think I'm pretty.

    1   2   3   4   5

I notice those who are "inside pretty" more than those with outer beauty.

    1   2   3   4   5

KEY

MOSTLY 1s Whoa! You have your priorities inside out. Ask God to help you work on that.

MOSTLY 2s You know you shouldn't, but you still put too much priority on looks. Pray for the right focus.

MOSTLY 3s Medium. You may want to be kind, but you still care a little too much about appearance.

MOSTLY 4s You're getting there. It's a tough journey, but you're going to make it.

MOSTLY 5s Congratulations! You have the right perspective on true beauty.

THINGS TO DO

- ◯ Make a list of the three things that make it toughest for you to let go of "outer beauty."

- ◯ Memorize 1 Peter 3:3-4.

- ◯ Think about someone you consider attractive. What is it that makes her attractive?

- ◯ Write down your best quality. Maybe it is kindness, compassion, humor, or helpfulness.

THINGS TO REMEMBER

Pay careful attention to your own work, for then you will get the satisfaction of a job well done, and you won't need to compare yourself to anyone else. **GALATIANS 6:4**

I knew you before I formed you in your mother's womb.
Before you were born I set you apart and appointed you as my prophet to the nations. **JEREMIAH 1:5**

The LORD said to Samuel, "Don't judge by his appearance or height, for I have rejected him. The LORD doesn't see things the way you see them. People judge by outward appearance, but the LORD looks at the heart." **1 SAMUEL 16:7**

Thank you for making me so wonderfully complex!
Your workmanship is marvelous— how well I know it. **PSALM 139:14**

Above all, clothe yourselves with love, which binds us all together in perfect harmony. **COLOSSIANS 3:14**

Develop interest in life as you see it; in people, things, literature, music—the world is so rich, simply throbbing with rich treasures, beautiful souls and interesting people. Forget yourself.
HENRY MILLER

Beauty, unaccompanied by virtue, is a flower without perfume.
PROVERB

Beauty is not in the face; Beauty is a light in the heart.
KAHLIL GIBRAN

Choose Your Path

No one can serve two masters. For you will hate one and love the other; you will be devoted to one and despise the other. You cannot serve both God and money.

MATTHEW 6:24

SELENA HAD DREAMS—big dreams. She wanted to become a famous softball pitcher. She was already good. She could whip the ball across the plate so fast that the batters hardly saw it fly by. She made the travel team even though she was a year younger than the other players. Her coach said she had a great future. But there was a problem . . . the travel team played on Sunday mornings. Selena's parents didn't think she should miss church to play softball. Selena didn't agree.

"I love God. I'm a Christian and all that, but I want to be a ballplayer. I have to play whenever I can!" she argued.

"Selena, God is the one who gave you the talent to play ball. He wants you to succeed, but Sunday morning is his time. You can play softball the other six and a half days of the week," Dad said.

Wow, this is tough. Selena's in danger of doing just what Matthew 6:24 warns against—trying to serve two masters. She wants to be the best ballplayer ever but still be true to what God wants.

It's okay to want to be the best at something. It's okay to give lots of time and energy to improving your skill. But

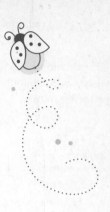

nothing—absolutely nothing—should ever be more important to you than God. If you let something else become that important, then you may start resenting God. Keep God in first place.

CHECKUP TIME

On a scale of 1 to 5, check where your priorities are.

1 = never
2 = not very often
3 = sometimes
4 = most of the time
5 = always

I choose to attend church regardless of what else is going on.

1   2   3   4   5

Knowing God and growing in faith are most important in my life.

1   2   3   4   5

Serving God comes ahead of anything else I enjoy.

1   2   3   4   5

I know that my talents are gifts from God.

1   2   3   4   5

I trust my parents' advice on this topic.

1   2   3   4   5

KEY

MOSTLY 1s You're in trouble. You'd better stop and examine your priorities.

MOSTLY 2s You're still confused about keeping God first in your life. Ask God to help you choose him, even if it means sacrificing something good.

MOSTLY 3s Looks like you're trying to ride the fence. You can't have both yourself *and* God in first place.

MOSTLY 4s Not bad, but you still need to fully commit to God. Ask him to help you with the things you have a hard time letting go of.

MOSTLY 5s Congratulations! You're keeping God number one in your life!

THINGS TO DO

- ○ Think about what activity or thing in your life tries to take God's place.

- ○ Memorize Matthew 6:24.

- ○ Ask an adult to help you figure out how to make time for what you want to do without pushing God out of the way.

- ○ Set a time every day to read your Bible and pray. Keep that date with God!

THINGS TO REMEMBER

What does the LORD your God require of you? He requires only that you fear the LORD your God, and live in a way that pleases him, and love him and serve him with all your heart and soul. **DEUTERONOMY 10:12**

As for me and my family, we will serve the LORD. **JOSHUA 24:15**

Seek the Kingdom of God above all else, and live righteously, and he will give you everything you need. **MATTHEW 6:33**

You must not bow down to [any idols or images of anything] or worship them, for I, the LORD your God, am a jealous God who will not tolerate your affection for any other gods. **EXODUS 20:5**

Come close to God, and God will come close to you. Wash your hands, you sinners; purify your hearts, for your loyalty is divided between God and the world. **JAMES 4:8**

Things which matter most must never be at the mercy of things which matter least.
JOHANN WOLFGANG VON GOETHE

Life without God is like an unsharpened pencil—it has no point.
BILLY GRAHAM

At the end of life we will not be judged by how many diplomas we have received, how much money we have made, how many great things we have done. We will be judged by "I was hungry and you gave me something to eat. I was naked and you clothed me. I was homeless and you took me in."
MOTHER TERESA

Pray for *Her*?

Bless those who persecute you. Don't curse them; pray that God will bless them.
ROMANS 12:14

ANNIE SLAMMED HER BOOKS DOWN on the kitchen table. "I wish Jillian would drop her books in front of the entire class—and that her pants would split when she goes to pick them up!" she shouted.

"Another bad day?" Mom asked. "I prayed that today would be better."

"Well, it wasn't. She made fun of me in front of the whole lunchroom . . . about something that isn't even true. Then, in the hallway, she pushed my books out of my arms and made a big deal of announcing what a clumsy dork I am," Annie said. "Why does she pick on me? She even makes fun of me because I believe in God. She says stuff like, 'Maybe God will send an angel to pick up your books' or 'Too bad God didn't help you ace the math test.' Mean, mean, mean!"

"Yeah, it is mean. Let's pray for Jillian—" Mom started to suggest, but Annie interrupted.

"Pray for *her*? Yeah, I'll pray that no one invites her to any parties this year. I'll pray that she forgets the answers on every one of her tests. I'll pray that everyone in the whole school realizes how awful she is."

"Annie. That's not what Romans 12:14 tells us to do. Give up the idea of getting even. God wants us to pray blessings on those who make our lives hard. Pray for Jillian to see his love through you. Pray for whatever is going on in her life that makes her behave the way she does," Mom said.

That's not easy, is it? When someone is mean to you, the natural reaction is to be mean back. But if you pray for the person who treats you badly, she may see God's love shining through you. That's the best thing that could happen— to her and to you.

If someone is bullying you, of course you should pray for her to be kinder and to be aware that she is hurting you. But it is also a good idea to tell an adult what's going on. A teacher or parent will be able to help you.

CHECKUP TIME

On a scale of 1 to 5, how do you handle people who are mean to you?

1 = never
2 = not very often
3 = sometimes
4 = most of the time
5 = always

I ask God to make good things happen for them.

1 2 3 4 5

I forgive them—even if they don't ask or care.

1 2 3 4 5

I look for ways to do nice things for them.

1 2 3 4 5

I keep quiet if it only happens occasionally; I don't gossip about them.

1 2 3 4 5

I give up the idea of getting even with them.

1 2 3 4 5

KEY

MOSTLY 1s It's hard to be picked on, but you're just making it worse by how you are responding. Commit to praying for the other person every day for a week and see if anything changes.

MOSTLY 2s You're obviously hurting. Talk to a parent or another trusted adult about a better way to handle your emotions.

MOSTLY 3s You've got the right idea; keep forgiving and moving forward.

MOSTLY 4s Hey, you are starting to see that the person who picks on you is a child of God too!

MOSTLY 5s Good job! Keep praying for your enemies. Ask God to show his love for them through you.

THINGS TO DO

○ Write out Romans 12:14 and put it somewhere that you will see it every day.

○ Make a list of kind things you can do for the person who picks on you.

○ Every time you think of something bad you would like to happen to the person who's picking on you, pray for her instead.

○ Ask an adult, such as your mom or a teacher you trust, to pray with you and for you about how to respond when someone picks on you.

THINGS TO REMEMBER

To you who are willing to listen, I say, love your enemies! Do good to those who hate you. LUKE 6:27

Love your enemies! Pray for those who persecute you! MATTHEW 5:44

I pray that your love will overflow more and more, and that you will keep on growing in knowledge and understanding. PHILIPPIANS 1:9

Don't repay evil for evil. Don't retaliate with insults when people insult you. Instead, pay them back with a blessing. That is what God has called you to do, and he will grant you his blessing. 1 PETER 3:9

Understand this, my dear brothers and sisters: You must all be quick to listen, slow to speak, and slow to get angry. Human anger does not produce the righteousness God desires. JAMES 1:19-20

An eye for an eye will only make the whole world blind.
GANDHI

Not forgiving is like drinking rat poison and then waiting for the rat to die.
ANNE LAMOTT

Do I not destroy my enemies when I make them my friends?
ABRAHAM LINCOLN

Cleaning Up

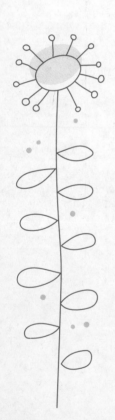

Create in me a clean heart, O God. Renew a loyal spirit within me.

PSALM 51:10

"YOU USED TO BE SO NICE. What happened?" Marki said.

Lucy didn't think she was acting any different than she ever had. She said to her friend Danielle, "Marki can't take the truth. It's her own fault that she acts like a geek and hangs out with total losers."

"Um, well, actually I think Marki is kind of right," Danielle said softly.

"What are you talking about?" Lucy shouted. "I'm the same as I've always been!"

"Not exactly. You've been acting sort of mean lately, especially with Marki. You really pick on her." Danielle was gentle but honest.

Lucy still didn't agree, but she couldn't stop thinking about what Danielle had said. *Am I different? Am I being mean?* she wondered. Lucy thought back over the last couple of weeks. To her surprise—and shame—she could think of things she had done and said that were not very nice.

Why did I start acting like this? she wondered. *And what am I going to do about it?*

Lucy has taken the first step—she recognizes the problem and is looking for the solution. She will quickly find out

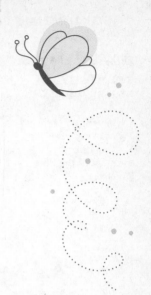

that there is only one answer. She needs to pray the prayer of Psalm 51:10, asking God to clean up her heart. He will help her turn around to thinking and behaving with kindness and love.

Sometimes unkindness or mean things sneak into your words and actions. It happens so slowly that you don't even notice. But once you recognize it, the best thing to do is ask God to help you clean up your heart so that your words and actions can show his love to others.

CHECKUP TIME

On a scale of 1 to 5, how well are you treating others?

1 = never
2 = not very often
3 = sometimes
4 = most of the time
5 = always

I notice how my words and actions make others feel.

1   2   3   4   5

I am respectful of others.

1   2   3   4   5

I try to obey God's teachings about loving others.

1   2   3   4   5

I listen when someone tells me I'm being unkind.

1   2   3   4   5

I'm willing to let God clean up my heart and make me more like him.

1   2   3   4   5

KEY

MOSTLY 1s You're not paying much attention to how you make others feel. Time for a turnaround!

MOSTLY 2s Your heart is still pretty dirty. Will you ask God to help you clean it up?

MOSTLY 3s You're not always unkind and disrespectful, but you still need some work.

MOSTLY 4s You're on the right path. Keep asking God for help with being kind.

MOSTLY 5s Good job! You know you need to let God clean up your heart, and you're letting him do it every day!

THINGS TO DO

○ You know yourself better than anyone else does. What do you need cleaned in your heart?

○ Memorize the prayer in Psalm 51:10. Pray it as often as you can.

○ Think of people you may need to apologize to for your unkind or disrespectful behavior.

○ Ask God's forgiveness—he is the one you hurt most when you are unkind.

THINGS TO REMEMBER

Let the Spirit renew your thoughts and attitudes. EPHESIANS 4:23

Stop acting so proud and haughty!
Don't speak with such arrogance!
For the LORD is a God who knows
what you have done;
he will judge your actions. 1 SAMUEL 2:3

Cling to your faith in Christ, and keep your conscience clear. For some people have deliberately violated their consciences; as a result, their faith has been shipwrecked. 1 TIMOTHY 1:19

No one has ever seen God. But if we love each other, God lives in us, and his love is brought to full expression in us. 1 JOHN 4:12

Since God chose you to be the holy people he loves, you must clothe yourselves with tenderhearted mercy, kindness, humility, gentleness, and patience. COLOSSIANS 3:12

Life is short. . . . Be swift to love, make haste to be kind!
HENRI F. AMIEL

The million little things that drop into our hands, the small opportunities that each day brings, God leaves us free to use or abuse—and goes unchanging along his silent way.
HELEN KELLER

Lord, whatever you want, wherever you want it, and whenever you want it, that's what I want.
DAVID JEREMIAH, PARAPHRASING RICHARD BAXTER

Building Up Muscle

Physical training is good, but training for godliness is much better, promising benefits in this life and in the life to come.

1 TIMOTHY 4:8

MORGAN STOOD BY the tennis courts and watched Beth play. Beth was awesome! She ran around the court returning balls, making it look so easy. She hardly ever missed one. One point went on so long that Morgan couldn't believe Beth was still running full strength. She didn't even seem tired! *How does she do it?* Morgan wondered.

Here's the thing: Beth loves sports—soccer, tennis, softball, swimming—just about any sport you can think of. She has seriously never found one she doesn't like . . . or one she isn't good at. One of the reasons Beth is so good is that she spends hours practicing and strengthening her muscles. She makes sure her body is in the best shape possible so that she can be a good athlete. She runs. She lifts weights. She eats right. She gets enough rest. Yeah, she is totally serious about being a good athlete.

Maybe you're a good athlete too. Or, maybe you're a musician or a writer or a cook or something else. If there is something that you love to do, you know that you have to work hard to be the best you can be. You must take seriously what is required of you. But here's something to think about: How seriously do you work on growing a stronger faith and becoming more like God in how you act, speak, and think? Is it something that you only give Sunday morning to? Do you only think about God when you go to church?

Growing into a strong, healthy God-follower takes some training too. This means reading your Bible every day to understand what it means to be like God; spending time talking with God and listening for his response each day; serving God by helping others. Being serious about growing in faith requires being serious about training— just like with anything else you want to be good at.

CHECKUP TIME

On a scale of 1 to 5, how are you doing with spiritual training?

1 = never
2 = not very often
3 = sometimes
4 = most of the time
5 = always

I am willing to do the work to gain the growth.

1   2   3   4   5

I take seriously learning how to become more like God.

1   2   3   4   5

I regularly spend time reading God's Word.

1   2   3   4   5

I put time with God ahead of other activities.

1   2   3   4   5

I ask God to help me become loving and kind like him.

1   2   3   4   5

KEY

MOSTLY 1s Check your priorities. You don't seem to be making spiritual training an important part of your life.

MOSTLY 2s You certainly don't give your full effort to this. What is one thing you can do this week to make spiritual training a bigger priority?

MOSTLY 3s Are you trying to ride the fence and have things both ways? Ask God to help you commit to growing in him.

MOSTLY 4s You're making a solid effort. Keep going!

MOSTLY 5s It's obviously important to you to grow stronger in your faith. Good job!

THINGS TO DO

○ Make a priority list of how you want to schedule your time each day.

○ Set a time when you will sit down alone and read your Bible every day.

○ Ask someone to hold you accountable to your daily time with God.

○ Memorize 1 Timothy 4:8.

THINGS TO REMEMBER

I pray that from his glorious, unlimited resources he will empower you with inner strength through his Spirit. Then Christ will make his home in your hearts as you trust in him. Your roots will grow down into God's love and keep you strong.
EPHESIANS 3:16-17

Let your roots grow down into him, and let your lives be built on him. Then your faith will grow strong in the truth you were taught, and you will overflow with thankfulness. **COLOSSIANS 2:7**

Let us stop going over the basic teachings about Christ again and again. Let us go on instead and become mature in our understanding. **HEBREWS 6:1**

All athletes are disciplined in their training. They do it to win a prize that will fade away, but we do it for an eternal prize.
1 CORINTHIANS 9:25

The LORD says, "I will guide you along the best pathway for your life. I will advise you and watch over you."
PSALM 32:8

Life is not worth living unless you live it for the One who gave you life.
ANYA VONDERLUFT

Faith is the muscle of the spirit. It is strengthened through study, prayer, and meditation. As exercise builds muscle and our bodies become strong; study, prayer, and meditation builds faith and our spirits become strong.
GERARD DE MARIGNY

A state of mind that sees God in everything is evidence of growth in grace and a thankful heart.
CHARLES FINNEY

Give thanks to the LORD, for he is good! His faithful love endures forever.

1 CHRONICLES 16:34

THE WATER OF THE LAKE was so still that it looked like a mirror. The snow-topped mountain behind it was reflected in the water. The sky was such a bright blue that it almost hurt Carla's eyes. *I've never seen anything so beautiful*, she thought. Later that afternoon Carla went on a hike with her family. As they hiked, they heard a roaring and crashing sound. When they came around a bend in the path, Carla saw the biggest, most powerful waterfall she had ever seen in person. It was awesome! Then her dad showed her a way she could climb around behind it and see the water crashing down from under a big rock. As they stood there together behind the waterfall, Carla's dad began to pray, "Thank you, Father, for this beautiful place you have created. Thank you for the time we have as a family to enjoy this. You thought of so many awesome things to make, things that demonstrate your love for us and your power and your creativity. I don't want to forget to say thanks."

Carla thought it was cool that her dad prayed right then. He did that a lot. His habit of thanking God right in the moment taught Carla to do the same thing. So when she saw a beautiful flower or noticed a colorful bird or giggled at her kitten's behavior, she often said, "Thanks," right out loud.

What about you? Do you remember to thank God for the things you enjoy every day? Those things all come from him, you know. Don't forget to thank him even for the things you might have been taking for granted, such as family, pets, friends, sunshine, rain, your home, or even your favorite treat.

CHECKUP TIME

On a scale of 1 to 5, how are you doing at remembering to thank God for all he gives?

1 = never
2 = not very often
3 = sometimes
4 = most of the time
5 = always

I can't help but thank God for the beauty I see in nature.

1   2   3   4   5

Saying thanks is at the front of my mind.

1   2   3   4   5

Even when I'm having a bad day, I thank God.

1   2   3   4   5

I encourage others to be thankful.

1   2   3   4   5

When I hear someone complaining, I point out something good they can be thankful for.

1   2   3   4   5

KEY

MOSTLY 1s Ugh. Your ungrateful attitude means you're probably not much fun to be around. Try to find three things today that you can be thankful for.

MOSTLY 2s Come on, you can do better. Make an effort to thank God and one other person for something they did for you this week.

MOSTLY 3s So-so. You could stand to work on being more thankful. What's good in your life? That's a gift from God!

MOSTLY 4s You do a good job of remembering to say thanks most of the time, but there's room for improvement. Find one new thing to be thankful for today!

MOSTLY 5s Good job! Your attitude of gratitude brings joy to your heart—and probably to the hearts of those around you too!

THINGS TO DO

- ◯ Make a list of things to be thankful for. Writing down a few things should open your eyes to more. You might find that it's hard to stop!

- ◯ Memorize a "thanks" verse and try to start each day by saying it out loud.

- ◯ Speak thankful words once each day—say aloud something you are thankful for. Thank the people in your life for what they give you or do for you.

- ◯ Tell God what your favorite thing is that he has made for you.

THINGS TO REMEMBER

O LORD my God, I will give you thanks forever! PSALM 30:12

Enter his gates with thanksgiving;
go into his courts with praise.
Give thanks to him and praise his name.
PSALM 100:4

Give thanks for everything to God the Father in the name of our Lord Jesus Christ.
EPHESIANS 5:20

Sing psalms and hymns and spiritual songs to God with thankful hearts. COLOSSIANS 3:16

Be thankful in all circumstances, for this is God's will for you who belong to Christ Jesus.
1 THESSALONIANS 5:18

If you want to turn your life around, try thankfulness. It will change your life mightily.
GERALD GOOD

Feeling gratitude and not expressing it is like wrapping a present and not giving it.
WILLIAM ARTHUR WARD

If we thanked God for the good things, there wouldn't be time to weep over the bad.
YIDDISH PROVERB

Kind Words Solve Problems

A gentle answer deflects anger, but harsh words make tempers flare.

PROVERBS 15:1

KESHIA'S BROTHER was driving her crazy! Everything he did annoyed her, frustrated her, made her mad. He was a nonstop pain in the neck. The *really* frustrating thing was that whenever he did something annoying and she yelled at him for it, Keshia's mom got mad at *her* because, of course, her brother yelled back, and pretty soon they were in a full-fledged war! Keshia couldn't win. How could she get her brother to leave her alone if she didn't yell at him to stop?

Mom saw what was going on. One day she sat Keshia down and gave her some advice. "Your brother can be a pain. I get it. But when you get mad and yell at him, then he gets mad and yells back, and well, it just goes on and on," she said.

"Yeah, I know," Keshia sighed. "What do I do?"

"Don't yell at him," Mom said. "You will get a better response by speaking softly and gently to him."

"You want me to be . . . nice?" Keshia asked. She couldn't believe what she was hearing.

"Yes," Mom said. "Angry words from you will boil the whole disagreement into a war. Gentle words will stop the war. It's in your hands."

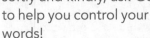

Keshia's mom is asking her to do something really hard, isn't she? Could you do it? When someone makes you mad, can you respond with kind and gentle words so the fight doesn't grow bigger? It isn't easy, that's for sure. But God says it is the right thing to do—it's the God thing to do. So if you need some help with speaking softly and kindly, ask God to help you control your words!

CHECKUP TIME

On a scale of 1 to 5, how are you doing with speaking kindly and gently?

1 = never
2 = not very often
3 = sometimes
4 = most of the time
5 = always

When someone speaks unkindly to me, I respond with gentleness.

   1   **2**   **3**   **4**   **5**

Keeping the peace is important to me.

   1   **2**   **3**   **4**   **5**

I can walk away from an argument.

   1   **2**   **3**   **4**   **5**

I ask God to help me be kind.

   1   **2**   **3**   **4**   **5**

Showing God's love is more important to me than getting the last word.

   1   **2**   **3**   **4**   **5**

KEY

MOSTLY 1s Yikes. Do you enjoy fights? Ask God to give you the heart of a peacemaker.

MOSTLY 2s Are you willing to work on this? Think of a strategy for not losing your temper, and commit to sticking to it.

MOSTLY 3s So-so, but you need to do better. Pick two of the action steps on the next page to work on this week.

MOSTLY 4s You're doing pretty well. Once in a while you give in to arguing, but not usually. Keep going!

MOSTLY 5s Great job! Loving others is more important to you than winning.

THINGS TO DO

○ Come up with a plan to help you not respond with anger—take a deep breath, count to ten, or even leave the room if you need to.

○ Memorize Proverbs 15:1 or another verse about keeping peace.

○ Ask a friend or parent to help you remember to speak softly and gently.

○ Ask God to help you remember to speak to others in the same way you would like to be spoken to.

THINGS TO REMEMBER

The tongue is a small thing that makes grand speeches. But a tiny spark can set a great forest on fire. JAMES 3:5

Don't use foul or abusive language. Let everything you say be good and helpful, so that your words will be an encouragement to those who hear them. EPHESIANS 4:29

Don't get involved in foolish, ignorant arguments that only start fights. A servant of the Lord must not quarrel but must be kind to everyone, be able to teach, and be patient with difficult people. 2 TIMOTHY 2:23-24

Fix your thoughts on what is true, and honorable, and right, and pure, and lovely, and admirable. Think about things that are excellent and worthy of praise. PHILIPPIANS 4:8

Love is patient and kind. Love is not jealous or boastful or proud or rude. It does not demand its own way. It is not irritable, and it keeps no record of being wronged. 1 CORINTHIANS 13:4-5

He who angers you conquers you.
ELIZABETH KENNY

Hot heads and cold hearts never solved anything.
BILLY GRAHAM

Speak when you are angry and you'll make the best speech you'll ever regret.
LAURENCE J. PETER

Never Alone

> [Lord,] you go before me and follow me. You place your hand of blessing on my head.
>
> PSALM 139:5

CAMRYN COULDN'T SLEEP. Her mind wouldn't relax. Her muscles were tense—in fact, her whole body was as stiff as a board. She was scared, and she felt totally alone. Camryn's parents were getting a divorce. She wasn't totally surprised, because they had been arguing and fighting for a long time. But it was kind of scary to think that she wouldn't see her dad every day. Camryn wondered if her mom would be able to pay the bills. She didn't know if she and Mom would have to move—away from friends and to a new school. *I can't talk to anyone about this. None of my close friends will understand, because they haven't been through it,* she thought. *I can't talk to Mom or Dad because they have enough to deal with. I've never felt so alone.*

If you've been through anything like this then you know how scary it is. But Camryn isn't really alone. God is with her. Just as Psalm 139:5 says, he goes before her and he follows behind. He knows what she is feeling, and he will comfort her and strengthen her.

God watches out for you, too. Isn't it comforting to know that God is there ahead of any problem you go through?

He knows about it before you do. Nothing surprises him. He is behind you too, cleaning up the mess that the situation may have left. He doesn't leave you alone to go through anything . . . ever.

CHECKUP TIME

On a scale of 1 to 5, how are you doing at believing God is always with you?

1 = never
2 = not very often
3 = sometimes
4 = most of the time
5 = always

When I'm worried or scared, my first thought is to turn to God.

1   2   3   4   5

I believe God knows everything that happens to me.

1   2   3   4   5

I trust God to take care of me.

1   2   3   4   5

When people comfort me, I recognize that God sent them to me.

1   2   3   4   5

Even in difficult, painful situations I believe God is with me.

1   2   3   4   5

KEY

MOSTLY 1s Whoa. No wonder you are scared. Your faith needs strengthening! Ask God to help you learn to trust him.

MOSTLY 2s You need to work on learning to trust God. Make a list of the reasons why you can count on him. Try to read it over every day.

MOSTLY 3s Maybe you believe with your head that God will take care of you, but trust hasn't reached your heart yet. Keep praying and thinking about God's trustworthy qualities.

MOSTLY 4s Learning to trust God no matter what takes time—you're doing well and making progress.

MOSTLY 5s What peace! You trust God and believe he is always with you.

THINGS TO DO

○ You'll never have peace until you believe and trust. Look up verses where God promises to be with you.

○ Memorize Psalm 139:5 and repeat it to yourself whenever you feel fear creeping in.

○ Tell someone you trust about how alone you feel. Ask that person to remind you every day that God knows everything you are dealing with.

○ Pray. Pray. Pray. Ask God to help you believe and trust in his love for you and his presence with you.

THINGS TO REMEMBER

Don't be afraid, for I am with you.
Don't be discouraged, for I am your God.
I will strengthen you and help you.
I will hold you up with my victorious right hand. ISAIAH 41:10

Even when I walk
through the darkest valley,
I will not be afraid,
for you are close beside me.
Your rod and your staff
protect and comfort me. PSALM 23:4

[Jesus said,] "Be sure of this: I am with you always, even to the end of the age."
MATTHEW 28:20

You love him even though you have never seen him. Though you do not see him now, you trust him; and you rejoice with a glorious, inexpressible joy. 1 PETER 1:8

The LORD is a shelter for the oppressed, a refuge in times of trouble. PSALM 9:9

If you put your trust in God, then you can enjoy your life while God is solving your problem.
JOYCE MEYER

Trust the past to God's mercy, the present to God's love, and the future to God's providence.
ST. AUGUSTINE

When you can't see God's hand, trust His heart.
EMILY FREEMAN

Forgiveness on Repeat

Even if that person wrongs you seven times a day and each time turns again and asks forgiveness, you must forgive.

LUKE 17:4

"UGHHHH. I can't believe it. Andrea has done it again! She lies about me and gets me into trouble with my friends," Mallory cried. For, like, the tenth time she had to explain to a friend that what Andrea had said was not true.

Mallory went to talk to Andrea. Andrea saw her coming and blurted out, "I'm sorry. I'm so sorry. I start talking and before I know it I'm saying things that I know aren't true. I stretch the truth, and I know it gets you into trouble. Please forgive me. Please? Will you?"

What was frustrating was that *this had happened before.* Every time Andrea got caught in a lie, she apologized and asked forgiveness. *How many times do I have to forgive her?* Mallory wondered.

Well, that's the question, isn't it? When is it okay to say, "No more forgiveness"? The answer to that is . . . never. Some things are easier to forgive than others. When you don't have the strength to forgive someone, ask God to help you. Think about it—he has a lot of experience in forgiving people over and over . . . in fact, he has that experience with *you.* Haven't you asked his forgiveness for doing the same things over and over? Yeah, most of us have.

So when you need to forgive someone *again*, ask God to help you do it. Then let him worry about dealing with that person's behavior. That's his job, not yours. Your job is to forgive and love. Just as God forgives and loves you . . . over and over.

CHECKUP TIME

On a scale of 1 to 5, how good are you at forgiving?

1 = never
2 = not very often
3 = sometimes
4 = most of the time
5 = always

I'm willing to forgive people over and over.

1   2   3   4   5

I ask God to forgive me repeatedly for the same things!

1   2   3   4   5

I want to show God's love to others.

1   2   3   4   5

I believe it's God's job to straighten other people up—not mine.

1   2   3   4   5

When I have trouble forgiving someone, I ask God to help.

1   2   3   4   5

KEY

MOSTLY 1s Forgiveness is not one of your strengths. But it's not optional for a Christian! Take some time today to think about how God has forgiven you, and ask him to help you learn to forgive others.

MOSTLY 2s You might have a "get-even" personality instead of a forgiving one, but you don't have to give in to it! Is there someone you're having trouble forgiving? Commit to praying for that person every day for a week, and see if your heart changes toward him or her.

MOSTLY 3s Sometimes you forgive, but you can do better. Keep asking for God's forgiveness power!

MOSTLY 4s Forgiving over and over isn't easy, but you're doing pretty well. Keep going!

MOSTLY 5s Good for you! You know you *are* forgiven, so you *do* forgive.

THINGS TO DO

○ Is there someone you need to forgive today?
   Ask God to help you do it.

○ Memorize a verse (or two!) about God's forgiveness.

○ Keep track of how often you ask God to forgive you for
   doing the same kind of thing over and over.

○ Think about how often others—your parents, friends, teachers,
   siblings—forgive you for your behavior or actions.

THINGS TO REMEMBER

Forgive us our sins,
as we have forgiven those who sin
against us. **MATTHEW 6:12**

If you are presenting a sacrifice at the altar in
the Temple and you suddenly remember that
someone has something against you, leave your
sacrifice there at the altar. Go and be reconciled
to that person. Then come and offer your
sacrifice to God. **MATTHEW 5:23-24**

Love prospers when a fault is forgiven,
but dwelling on it separates close friends.
PROVERBS 17:9

If we confess our sins to him, he is faithful and
just to forgive us our sins and to cleanse us
from all wickedness. **1 JOHN 1:9**

"Come now, let's settle this," says the LORD.
"Though your sins are like scarlet,
I will make them as white as snow.
Though they are red like crimson,
I will make them as white as wool."
ISAIAH 1:18

*Let us forgive each
other. Only then will
we live in peace.*
LEO TOLSTOY

*The weak can never
forgive. Forgiveness
is the attribute of
the strong.*
GANDHI

*Forgiveness is an act
of the will, and the will
can function regardless
of the temperature of
the heart.*
CORRIE TEN BOOM

They're Watching

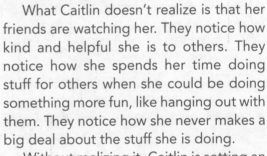

You yourself must be an example to them by doing good works of every kind. Let everything you do reflect the integrity and seriousness of your teaching.

TITUS 2:7

CAITLIN WENT next door to Mrs. Howard's house and spent the afternoon pulling weeds from the older woman's flower garden, just like she does every Tuesday afternoon. On Thursday afternoons she volunteers at a day care, reading stories to the children. Caitlin loves helping people and is always looking for new ways to help someone out. She doesn't brag about helping others; in fact, she doesn't really even talk about it. She just does it.

What Caitlin doesn't realize is that her friends are watching her. They notice how kind and helpful she is to others. They notice how she spends her time doing stuff for others when she could be doing something more fun, like hanging out with them. They notice how she never makes a big deal about the stuff she is doing.

Without realizing it, Caitlin is setting an example of service to her friends. They see her doing kind things for others. They see the joy she gets from it. Caitlin's friends know that she is a Christian and see by her service that she is an example of loving others the way that God says his followers should.

If your friends watch how you spend your time, do they see a good example of how to love and care for others? Are you showing God's love by how you live? Be careful . . . they're watching.

CHECKUP TIME

On a scale of 1 to 5, what kind of example are you?

1 = never
2 = not very often
3 = sometimes
4 = most of the time
5 = always

I spend time and energy doing things for others.

1 2 3 4 5

I try to live for Christ because I know others are watching.

1 2 3 4 5

I'm happy to serve others, even by doing things I don't really enjoy.

1 2 3 4 5

I watch how older Christians live so I can learn from them.

1 2 3 4 5

I ask God to help me be a good example.

1 2 3 4 5

KEY

MOSTLY 1s Ouch! We can only hope no one is watching your example! Ask God to make you aware of how your priorities reflect on him.

MOSTLY 2s You could use some help. Maybe you should find someone whose example you can follow.

MOSTLY 3s You try to serve others, but you still struggle with thinking only of yourself sometimes. Ask God to give you opportunities to put others first.

MOSTLY 4s Being a good example is pretty important to you. Keep working hard!

MOSTLY 5s Good job! You're a great example of God's love for others to see.

THINGS TO DO

○ Look around your family or your neighborhood for ways you can serve others.

○ Make a list of ways to show God's love to others.

○ Do some of the things on the list you made. Try to do at least one a week.

○ Ask God to help you see places to help others—opportunities you haven't noticed before.

THINGS TO REMEMBER

Don't let anyone think less of you because you are young. Be an example to all believers in what you say, in the way you live, in your love, your faith, and your purity. **1 TIMOTHY 4:12**

You should imitate me, just as I imitate Christ. **1 CORINTHIANS 11:1**

Whoever wants to be first among you must become your slave. For even the Son of Man came not to be served but to serve others and to give his life as a ransom for many. **MATTHEW 20:27-28**

Give your bodies to God because of all he has done for you. Let them be a living and holy sacrifice—the kind he will find acceptable. This is truly the way to worship him. **ROMANS 12:1**

If you try to hang on to your life, you will lose it. But if you give up your life for [Jesus'] sake, you will save it. **MATTHEW 16:25**

What you do speaks so loud that I cannot hear what you say.
RALPH WALDO EMERSON

We are the Bibles the world is reading; we are the creeds the world is needing; we are the sermons the world is heeding.
BILLY GRAHAM

Where one man reads the Bible, a hundred read you and me.
D. L. MOODY

When in Doubt . . .
Don't Do It!

If you have doubts about whether or not you should eat something, you are sinning if you go ahead and do it. For you are not following your convictions. If you do anything you believe is not right, you are sinning.
ROMANS 14:23

MELISSA HANDED LYNNIE A NOTE as they passed each other in the hallway. It said, "Meet us by the water fountain after school. We'll have some fun!" Lynnie was curious but also kind of anxious about meeting Melissa and her group of friends. They were the prettiest and most popular girls in school, but sometimes they did things that Lynnie didn't think were very nice.

After school she went to the water fountain. Melissa and five other girls were already there. "What's up?" Lynnie asked.

"We have a plan," Melissa said. She spoke so softly that Lynnie had to get in the center of the group to hear. "We are going to totally get Camie. She thinks she is so cool. We're tired of her being so stuck up and snotty. We've got the phone numbers of a bunch of the older kids, and we're gonna text them stuff about her and—"

"Um, hold on," Lynnie said. It took all of her courage to interrupt Melissa. "That sounds really mean. Is the stuff you're going to say even true?"

"Oh, don't be such a baby. Stick with us on this or *you* may be the one we get next!" Melissa said.

Yikes. What should Lynnie do? She believes that the things Melissa and her group are planning to do are wrong. So if she goes along with them, she is sinning, at least according to Romans 14:23.

If you know something is wrong but you go ahead and do it—to keep the peace with your friends, to fit in, or just because you're lazy—it's sin. Simple as that. When you know the right thing to do . . . do it. When you're not sure if something is right or wrong . . . don't do it!

CHECKUP TIME

On a scale of 1 to 5, how strong are you at resisting sin?

1 = never
2 = not very often
3 = sometimes
4 = most of the time
5 = always

I'm comfortable telling my friends no if I'm not sure about something.

1   2   3   4   5

I take sin seriously, and I try to avoid it.

1   2   3   4   5

I try to stop my friends from doing things I believe are wrong.

1   2   3   4   5

I pay attention when my heart or my conscience says something is wrong.

1   2   3   4   5

I ask God to help me be strong and avoid sin.

1   2   3   4   5

KEY

MOSTLY 1s You seem to have all the strength of a wet noodle! Ask God to help you stand firm.

MOSTLY 2s You don't seem to understand the seriousness of sin. Take some time to read in the Bible what God thinks about it.

MOSTLY 3s Sometimes you say no to doing wrong, and sometimes you say yes. Pray that God will help you say no consistently.

MOSTLY 4s You understand that sin is wrong. Keep asking God for the strength to resist it.

MOSTLY 5s Great strength! You listen to your heart and try to obey God.

THINGS TO DO

○ Read the story of Jesus' arrest and crucifixion. He went through all that to save you from the eternal consequences of your sin.

○ Promise yourself and God that you will take responsibility for your own actions. Ask God to help you remember and keep your commitment.

○ Memorize verses about the price of sin and your responsibility.

○ Ask God to help you to be strong so that you can resist when you know something is wrong.

THINGS TO REMEMBER

Put on your new nature, and be renewed as you learn to know your Creator and become like him. **COLOSSIANS 3:10**

I have hidden your word in my heart, that I might not sin against you. **PSALM 119:11**

Humble yourselves before God. Resist the devil, and he will flee from you. Come close to God, and God will come close to you. Wash your hands, you sinners; purify your hearts, for your loyalty is divided between God and the world. **JAMES 4:7-8**

If we confess our sins to him, he is faithful and just to forgive us our sins and to cleanse us from all wickedness. **1 JOHN 1:9**

The wages of sin is death, but the free gift of God is eternal life through Christ Jesus our Lord. **ROMANS 6:23**

No sin is small. It is a sin against an infinite God, and may have consequences immeasurable. No grain of sand is small in the mechanism of a watch.
JEREMY TAYLOR

One leak will sink a ship; and one sin will destroy a sinner.
JOHN BUNYAN

You win or lose by the way you choose.
UNKNOWN

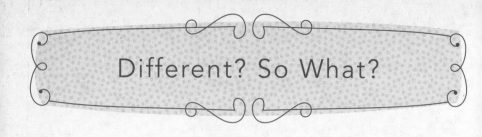

Different? So What?

I was hungry, and you fed me. I was thirsty, and you gave me a drink. I was a stranger, and you invited me into your home.
MATTHEW 25:35

THE FIRST DAY OF SCHOOL! Mia was really excited. She and her friends all laughed and talked at once about their busy summers. Mia was so caught up in the excitement that it took a while before she noticed a girl standing off to the side— alone. No one was talking with her. She looked . . . different. She wasn't wearing the same kinds of clothes as Mia and her friends. She had a different kind of hairstyle. Not better or worse—just different. She was obviously new to the school and probably even new to the country. She looked confused and a little scared.

At lunchtime, when Mia went to sit with her friends, she saw the new girl again. She looked more confused than ever. Mia almost walked right by her, but at the last minute she stopped and turned to the girl. "Hi, my name is Mia. What's yours?" she asked.

At first the girl looked shocked that someone was speaking to her, then hesitantly, almost in a whisper, she said, "Jamila."

"That's a pretty name. Do you want to eat lunch with my friends and me?" Mia asked. Jamila gladly joined the group of girls. Slowly she was able to explain that she was from an African country. Her family had to leave because of war. She didn't know much English, and she didn't know anyone at school.

"Well, you know someone now," Mia said. Everyone smiled.

Mia is living out what Jesus talked about in Matthew 25:35. She reached out to someone who was different, someone who was a stranger, and she made her a friend. That's what Jesus wants you to do!

On a scale of 1 to 5, how comfortable are you with reaching out to new people?

1 = never
2 = not very often
3 = sometimes
4 = most of the time
5 = always

I make an effort to talk to new people.

1   2   3   4   5

If I notice someone alone, I invite them into my group of friends.

1   2   3   4   5

I like to meet people from other countries and learn about their lives.

1   2   3   4   5

I think it's sad that people have to leave their homes because of war.

1   2   3   4   5

Even if it makes me uncomfortable to talk to someone who doesn't understand my language very well, I try to do it anyway.

1   2   3   4   5

KEY

MOSTLY 1s Hmm. You're not too good at reaching out to those who are different. Ask God to give you the courage to step outside your comfort zone.

MOSTLY 2s You have some work to do, my friend. Don't let nervousness or embarrassment get in the way!

MOSTLY 3s Not bad, but you can do better. Try reaching out to one new person this week.

MOSTLY 4s You're showing some care to those who are different. Keep up the good work!

MOSTLY 5s Good for you! You are showing Christ's love through your kindness.

THINGS TO DO

○ Look around at school, at church, or in your neighborhood. Are there girls your age who are new to this country? Take one step forward to talk with one of those girls.

○ Teach your new friend some helpful English words. Learn some words of her language.

○ Recruit some of your friends to help you reach out to someone new. It will be less uncomfortable if you all do it together!

○ If this is all kind of scary, ask God to help you.

THINGS TO REMEMBER

Don't forget to show hospitality to strangers, for some who have done this have entertained angels without realizing it! **HEBREWS 13:2**

Do to others whatever you would like them to do to you. **MATTHEW 7:12**

If I gave everything I have to the poor and even sacrificed my body, I could boast about it; but if I didn't love others, I would have gained nothing. **1 CORINTHIANS 13:3**

[Jesus said,] "Now I am giving you a new commandment: Love each other. Just as I have loved you, you should love each other." **JOHN 13:34**

No one has ever seen God. But if we love each other, God lives in us, and his love is brought to full expression in us. **1 JOHN 4:12**

Do not waste time bothering whether you "love" your neighbor; act as if you did.
C. S. LEWIS

Have you ever noticed how much of Christ's life was spent in doing kind things?
HENRY DRUMMOND

It is not how much you do but how much love you put into the doing and sharing with others that is important.
MOTHER TERESA

Crippled by Fear

Don't be afraid, for I am with you. Don't be discouraged, for I am your God.

I will strengthen you and help you. I will hold you up with my victorious right hand.

ISAIAH 41:10

STEPHANIE NEEDED SOMEONE to tell her that things were going to be okay. Someone she trusted. But no one could do that, because no one knew what was going to happen. Stephanie's older sister had just gotten in trouble—big trouble. Stephanie adored Lizzie. She looked up to her. She wanted to be like her. She tried to dress like Lizzie and do her hair like Lizzie's and copy anything else of Lizzie's she could.

Lizzie had gotten in trouble for selling drugs. Stephanie couldn't believe it. She *didn't* believe it. Now Lizzie was at the police station. Their parents were there too. Lizzie would probably not be home tonight. *What are we going to do? What's going to happen to Lizzie? What will I do without Lizzie around? I don't think I can do this. I can't believe this is all happening.* Stephanie was scared—scared for Lizzie, scared for herself, scared for their family. She felt too embarrassed to talk to anyone about it. She felt so alone.

Everyone gets scared at times. Sometimes you feel like no one understands or even cares. But you know what? That's not true—as Isaiah 41:10 says, God is with you. Always. He promised. While that's not the same as someone who can actually give you a hug, it is good to know that he is right there with you. Talk to him. Tell him how you feel. Ask him for comfort and strength—you can even ask him to send someone to give you that hug. Remember his promise. You are *not* alone.

CHECKUP TIME

On a scale of 1 to 5, how do you handle fear?

1 = never
2 = not very often
3 = sometimes
4 = most of the time
5 = always

I am comforted that God is always with me.

1   2   3   4   5

The first thing I do when I'm scared is pray.

1   2   3   4   5

I believe God has everything under control.

1   2   3   4   5

When I'm scared I try to remember the times God has helped me in the past.

1   2   3   4   5

I know that just because I feel alone doesn't mean I *am* alone.

1   2   3   4   5

KEY

MOSTLY 1s You need to work on your trust and belief in God's promises. Read one of the verses on the next page each day for a week. Read it slowly several times to let it really sink in.

MOSTLY 2s You've got some work to do in learning to trust God. Ask God to help you remember to run to him when you feel afraid.

MOSTLY 3s You're still struggling a bit. Maybe it would help to talk with someone about your fear.

MOSTLY 4s You're learning to take your fears to God. Keep moving forward.

MOSTLY 5s Hey, great job! You know God is always there for you.

THINGS TO DO

- ○ You gotta start somewhere. Choose one little thing to trust God with—then do it. Don't worry about it at all.
- ○ Write down times you know God has helped you in the past.
- ○ Memorize a verse about God being with you, like Isaiah 41:10. Say it every time you feel scared.
- ○ Talk with someone you trust and tell that person about your fears. Talking about it may help.

THINGS TO REMEMBER

God is our refuge and strength, always ready to help in times of trouble. So we will not fear when earthquakes come and the mountains crumble into the sea. **PSALM 46:1-2**

In peace I will lie down and sleep, for you alone, O LORD, will keep me safe. **PSALM 4:8**

Don't let your hearts be troubled. Trust in God, and trust also in me. **JOHN 14:1**

The LORD is my rock, my fortress, and my savior; my God is my rock, in whom I find protection. He is my shield, the power that saves me, and my place of safety. **PSALM 18:2**

Be strong and courageous! Do not be afraid and do not panic before them. For the LORD your God will personally go ahead of you. He will neither fail you nor abandon you. **DEUTERONOMY 31:6**

The presence of fear does not mean you have no faith. Fear visits everyone. But make your fear a visitor and not a resident.
MAX LUCADO

Though our feelings come and go, His love for us does not.
C. S. LEWIS

I must first have the sense of God's possession of me before I can have the sense of His presence with me.
WATCHMAN NEE

Hidden Motives

"DEAR GOD, let me be chosen for the mission trip to Chicago . . . uh . . . want to . . . uh . . . tell people about you and uh . . . do stuff for them. Amen," Reilly prayed. Only four kids her age would be chosen to go on the trip to Chicago, and Reilly wanted very much to be on the team. But her motives weren't really so spiritual. She didn't care about telling others about God. She wasn't willing to do some of the hard work that the team was scheduled to do. So why *did* Reilly want to go? She wanted to impress the other girls her age by being chosen. She was hoping to make them jealous of her. She was trying to show off. That's not the best motive for going on a mission trip, is it?

Reilly could pray all day for God to give her what she wanted, but her motives were all wrong. She didn't care about doing God's work; she cared about getting what she wanted. You won't be surprised to hear that Reilly was not chosen for the trip. She needed to get her priorities straightened out.

What about you? When you ask God for things, are you asking with the right motives? Are your prayers concerned with doing good for other people, with advancing God's work, with showing love and care? Or are you praying just to get stuff you want? Don't expect God to answer your prayers if you've got hidden motives. Be pure in your motives and in your prayer requests.

CHECKUP TIME

On a scale of 1 to 5, how would you score your motives?

1 = never
2 = not very often
3 = sometimes
4 = most of the time
5 = always

I try to put others first.
1   2   3   4   5

My main concern is that God's work gets done.
1   2   3   4   5

I want others to know that Christ is my motivation.
1   2   3   4   5

What others think about me is no big deal.
1   2   3   4   5

I let go of my desire to do whatever I want to do.
1   2   3   4   5

KEY

MOSTLY 1s If you're praying with these kinds of motives, you are probably going to be disappointed. Ask God to turn your heart around—toward him.

MOSTLY 2s Your priorities are still pretty upside down. Remember that being in line with what God wants is ultimately best for you, too.

MOSTLY 3s Middle of the road—you can do better than that. Check your heart when you pray. Change your prayers to be less you-focused.

MOSTLY 4s Pretty good, but maybe once in a while you still get in the way of God's work. Ask God to keep softening your heart.

MOSTLY 5s Good for you! You have good priorities and no hidden motives.

THINGS TO DO

○ Write down what you've been praying for lately. What's your honest motive for each of those prayers?

○ Think of the last few times when God has answered your prayers. What were your motives then?

○ Ask God to help you keep your priorities in the right order so that his work is most important to you.

○ Memorize a verse on good motives, such as Deuteronomy 10:12-13.

THINGS TO REMEMBER

What does the LORD your God require of you? He requires only that you fear the LORD your God, and live in a way that pleases him, and love him and serve him with all your heart and soul. And you must always obey the LORD's commands and decrees that I am giving you today for your own good.
DEUTERONOMY 10:12-13

Many who are the greatest now will be least important then, and those who seem least important now will be the greatest then.
MARK 10:31

Anyone who becomes as humble as this little child is the greatest in the Kingdom of Heaven.
MATTHEW 18:4

Watch out! Don't do your good deeds publicly, to be admired by others, for you will lose the reward from your Father in heaven. **MATTHEW 6:1**

Don't be selfish; don't try to impress others. Be humble, thinking of others as better than yourselves. **PHILIPPIANS 2:3**

A man wrapped up in himself makes a very small bundle.
BENJAMIN FRANKLIN

Selfishness is never so exquisitely selfish as when it is on its knees. . . . Self turns what would otherwise be a pure and powerful prayer into a weak and ineffective one.
A. W. TOZER

Man sees your actions, but God your motives.
THOMAS À KEMPIS

God's Got This!

When you pray, don't babble on and on as the Gentiles do. They think their prayers are answered merely by repeating their words again and again. Don't be like them, for your Father knows exactly what you need even before you ask him!

MATTHEW 6:7-8

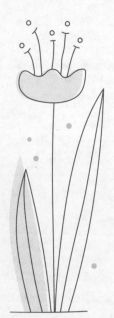

"MAKE IT STOP. Make it stop," Dara prays. Over and over. Those are the only words she can think of; she just doesn't know what else to ask. What do you pray for when your world is falling apart? Dara's parents are getting divorced. She and her mom and brother are going to live with Dara's grandparents—in another state. Everything is changing, and Dara is scared. She is angry. She is sad. She doesn't even know what to pray for except for God to make everything stop—and go back to the way things used to be when her family was happy.

Don't misunderstand—Dara does believe in God, and she does believe that prayer makes a difference. But she doesn't know what she needs to help her get through this. That's okay, though, because God already knows what she needs. He knows how much she is hurting. He knows how scared she is. He knows what the future holds. He knows how to answer prayers that she doesn't even know how to pray.

Isn't it wonderful that God knows what you need—even before you know? Sometimes life gets so confusing that your prayers become repetitive and you

feel like your requests cancel each other out because you don't really know what you want. That's okay. The bottom line is that God loves you, so trust him to know what you need. Ask him to do his will and to stay close to you through the journey. He will.

CHECKUP TIME

On a scale of 1 to 5, how much do you trust God to know your needs?

1 = never
2 = not very often
3 = sometimes
4 = most of the time
5 = always

I'm content to pray, "Your will, not mine, be done."

1   2   3   4   5

I accept God's will, even when it's hard.

1   2   3   4   5

I trust God to know what's best.

1   2   3   4   5

I believe that God will help me, even if I don't always know exactly what to pray for.

1   2   3   4   5

I believe in the power of prayer.

1   2   3   4   5

KEY

MOSTLY 1s It's kind of scary to feel like you have to be in control of everything in your life, isn't it? Ask God to help you let him take over.

MOSTLY 2s You know what trust is, but you need some help applying it to your life. Write out a verse about trusting God and put it somewhere where you'll see it every day.

MOSTLY 3s Average—you can do better! The more you choose to trust God, the more naturally it will come to you.

MOSTLY 4s You trust most of the time but not always. Ask God to help you deal with those areas of your life where you're still holding on to control.

MOSTLY 5s Congratulations! You understand God's love for you, and you trust him with your life.

THINGS TO DO

○ Pick the most confusing situation on your prayer list right now and give it to God.

○ Make a list of the ways God has taken care of you in the past—ways that you didn't expect but were exactly right.

○ Memorize some verses about trusting God.

○ Ask a trusted friend to pray with you for your faith to grow stronger.

THINGS TO REMEMBER

Don't worry about anything; instead, pray about everything. Tell God what you need, and thank him for all he has done. Then you will experience God's peace, which exceeds anything we can understand. His peace will guard your hearts and minds as you live in Christ Jesus. **PHILIPPIANS 4:6-7**

If you need wisdom, ask our generous God, and he will give it to you. He will not rebuke you for asking. **JAMES 1:5**

May your Kingdom come soon.
May your will be done on earth,
as it is in heaven. **MATTHEW 6:10**

Give all your worries and cares to God, for he cares about you. **1 PETER 5:7**

The LORD says, "I will guide you along the best pathway for your life. I will advise you and watch over you." **PSALM 32:8**

Teach me to treat all that comes to me throughout the day with peace of soul, and with the firm conviction that Your will governs all. Amen.
ORTHODOX PRAYER

All I have seen teaches me to trust the Creator for all I have not seen.
RALPH WALDO EMERSON

In the darkest of nights cling to the assurance that God loves you, that He always has advice for you, a path that you can tread and a solution to your problem—and you will experience that which you believe. God never disappoints anyone who places his [or her] trust in Him.
BASILEA SCHLINK

Watch It!

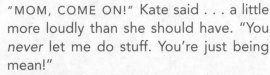

Stop being angry!
Turn from your rage!

Do not lose
your temper—
it only leads to harm.
PSALM 37:8

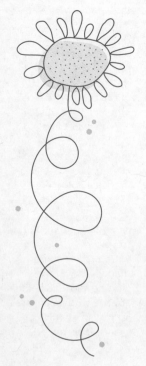

"MOM, COME ON!" Kate said . . . a little more loudly than she should have. "You *never* let me do stuff. You're just being mean!"

"Kate, be careful what you say to me," Mom said, "and watch your tone of voice."

"Why do I have to watch what I say? Why do I have to watch my tone? The problem is that you make too many rules. Why do you treat me like a little kid? Why won't you let me do the stuff that my friends get to do? This isn't fair! You're just ruining my life!" Kate was screaming by the time she finished speaking. She was completely out of control.

If you've ever been in a "conversation" like this with your mom or dad, you know that this is not going to end well for Kate. It's probably going to end with her getting grounded or punished in some other way. It's a proven fact that losing your temper only leads to trouble. God knows that, which is why he warns us in Psalm 37:8 against giving in to anger.

You know how temper works—when you're having a disagreement with someone, losing your temper only makes things worse. When you get mad, you say things you don't really mean and do things that hurt others. The goal for a Christian is to become more and more like Jesus. You can't be a good example of his love when you're filled with anger.

CHECKUP TIME

On a scale of 1 to 5, how well do you control your anger?

1 = never
2 = not very often
3 = sometimes
4 = most of the time
5 = always

I keep my cool pretty easily.

   1   2   3   4   5

I am careful not to say things I'll regret.

   1   2   3   4   5

I respect others' opinions.

   1   2   3   4   5

I ask people I trust to give me a signal when I'm about to lose my temper.

   1   2   3   4   5

I know I deserve correction when I "lose it."

   1   2   3   4   5

KEY

MOSTLY 1s Temper, temper! Yeah, you need to work on yours. But don't be discouraged—there's no temper too hot for God to change.

MOSTLY 2s Not the worst, for sure. But you still need to improve. Talk to your parents or another trusted adult about some strategies for keeping it cool.

MOSTLY 3s Average. Ask God to help you not to sin when you get angry.

MOSTLY 4s So, you usually control your temper. Still room for improvement, though—don't stop now!

MOSTLY 5s Good job. You have a handle on your angry emotions!

THINGS TO DO

○ Apologize to someone who has been the victim of one of your temper outbursts.

○ Next time you are about to lose your temper, stop. Count to ten. Try to see things from a different viewpoint. (Ask God to help you remember to do this!)

○ Memorize some verses that help you keep your temper in line.

○ Pray. Ask God to help you keep your temper under control.

THINGS TO REMEMBER

Human anger does not produce the righteousness God desires. **JAMES 1:20**

Work at living in peace with everyone, and work at living a holy life, for those who are not holy will not see the Lord. **HEBREWS 12:14**

Among all the parts of the body, the tongue is a flame of fire. It is a whole world of wickedness, corrupting your entire body. It can set your whole life on fire, for it is set on fire by hell itself. **JAMES 3:6**

"Don't sin by letting anger control you." Don't let the sun go down while you are still angry. **EPHESIANS 4:26**

You have heard that our ancestors were told, "You must not murder. If you commit murder, you are subject to judgment." But I say, if you are even angry with someone, you are subject to judgment! If you call someone an idiot, you are in danger of being brought before the court. And if you curse someone, you are in danger of the fires of hell. **MATTHEW 5:21-22**

If you kick a stone in anger, you'll hurt your own foot.
KOREAN PROVERB

Whatever is begun in anger ends in shame.
BENJAMIN FRANKLIN

Anger is an acid that can do more harm to the vessel in which it is stored than to anything on which it is poured.
MARK TWAIN

What Now?

TALIA IS A BUSY GIRL. Between school, piano lessons, and soccer, she hardly has a free minute! But the director of creative arts at her church has asked her to join the team. It looks like a lot of fun. They do programs using music, drama, and visual art, and Talia loves that. She has a good voice, so she would be able to sing with them. The thing is, the team practices one evening a week. They do programs at other churches and schools and camps. They travel in the summer. Being a member of the team takes a lot of time! Talia isn't sure where she will find the time, at least without giving up something else.

Talia talked to her parents about the decision. They agree that she has to make a choice. There are pros and cons. She is a good soccer player—good enough that she might get a scholarship to college someday. But the creative arts team is a chance to be a part of a wonderful ministry. She can be a missionary to her soccer teammates, but she can be a ministry partner with the creative arts teammates.

Aaaahhh! What to do? Talia knows the most important thing to do—pray. She believes God will guide her. Smart girl, that Talia.

God has plans that are so big, we can't begin to understand them. He wants his followers to be in certain places at certain times to do his work. He cares about his followers using the talents he gave them. So if you have a question about what to do, how to spend your time, or where to put your energy, just ask him. He'll direct you. He said he would.

CHECKUP TIME

On a scale of 1 to 5, how much do you seek God's guidance?

1 = never
2 = not very often
3 = sometimes
4 = most of the time
5 = always

When I have a decision to make, the first thing I do is pray.

    1   2   3   4   5

I want to know what God's plans are for me.

    1   2   3   4   5

I listen for God to speak to me through the advice of people I trust.

    1   2   3   4   5

I'm good at waiting until I'm sure God has given me guidance.

    1   2   3   4   5

I'm willing to let go of something I enjoy if God directs me that way.

    1   2   3   4   5

KEY

MOSTLY 1s We get it—you like to do things *your* way. But God's way is actually better for you. Ask him to help you believe that.

MOSTLY 2s Could it be that you don't trust God to guide you? Ask your parents or your pastor to help you find some Bible verses that speak to that.

MOSTLY 3s You're about fifty-fifty. Sometimes you pray for guidance and sometimes not. Think of something you could use as a reminder to do it all the time.

MOSTLY 4s So maybe you ask God for guidance but aren't so good at waiting for his answer? Ask him for patience!

MOSTLY 5s Good job. Your faith is strong, and you trust God's will for your life.

THINGS TO DO

○ Make a list of decisions for which you need God's guidance.

○ Pray about one of the things on your list. Commit to waiting for God's direction.

○ Write out a favorite verse about trusting God. Put it where you will see it every day.

○ Ask a trusted friend to pray with you for God's guidance.

THINGS TO REMEMBER

The LORD directs the steps of
the godly.
He delights in every detail of their lives.
Though they stumble, they will never fall,
for the LORD holds them by the hand.
PSALM 37:23-24

Seek his will in all you do,
and he will show you which path to take.
PROVERBS 3:6

"I know the plans I have for you," says the
LORD. "They are plans for good and not for
disaster, to give you a future and a hope."
JEREMIAH 29:11

The LORD is good to those who depend on him,
to those who search for him.
LAMENTATIONS 3:25

You saw me before I was born.
Every day of my life was recorded in your book.
Every moment was laid out
before a single day had passed.
PSALM 139:16

It's incredible to realize that what we do each day has meaning in the big picture of God's plan.
BILL HYBELS

In the center of a hurricane there is absolute peace and quiet. There is no safer place than in the center of the will of God.
CORRIE TEN BOOM

Knowing where you are going takes the uncertainty out of getting there.
ANNE GRAHAM LOTZ

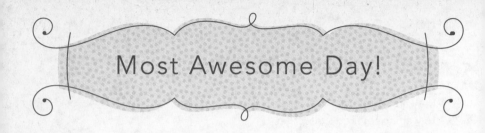

Most Awesome Day!

Let everything that breathes sing praises to the LORD! Praise the LORD!

PSALM 150:6

MADDIE FELT LIKE SKIPPING and singing and laughing and, well, all of those at once. She was filled with joy. It was just one of those days where everywhere she looked, she saw something amazing.

The sky was super blue with white, fluffy clouds in it. The flowers around Maddie's house were brilliant pops of color. Her kitten was doing silly things that made her laugh. She saw her teenage neighbor helping their elderly neighbor and making the woman smile with whatever he was saying to her. Maddie's mom was singing while she worked in the garden. Maddie's baby brother was giggling at a toy. It was just a perfect day. It felt like everything on earth was stretching up toward heaven to say with Maddie, "Thanks, God, for this perfect day!"

Maddie gets it! She is giving God the praise for all that is around her and all that she is enjoying.

The days when everything goes well and you are filled with joy just don't seem to come often enough, do they? Sometimes, you must make the choice to be joyful, even if things aren't perfect. Just stop, look around, and see what you can find to praise God for. There will be something, for sure. Every beautiful thing you see around you. Everything you have. Every person you know. Every pet you enjoy. All of it is from God. He shows his love for you each day by what he has made for you to enjoy. And all creation praises him for it.

On a scale of 1 to 5, how are you doing at praising God?

1 = never
2 = not very often
3 = sometimes
4 = most of the time
5 = always

Each day, I notice stuff that God does for me.

1   2   3   4   5

I take time to say, "Thanks" to him.

1   2   3   4   5

I make sure to praise him in front of others so they will be reminded to praise him too.

1   2   3   4   5

I like to let my joy show to everyone!

1   2   3   4   5

Even on bad days, I can find things to thank God for.

1   2   3   4   5

KEY

MOSTLY 1s Whoa. There's not a lot of joy in that heart of yours! Read Psalm 30:11, which talks about God turning mourning into joy. Ask him to do that for you.

MOSTLY 2s You need to do a "praise" workout. Find at least five things today that you can praise God for.

MOSTLY 3s You're doing okay, but you can do better for sure. Keep practicing praise!

MOSTLY 4s Don't let even occasional grumpiness push aside your joy. Press on until thanking God is as natural as breathing!

MOSTLY 5s Awesome! You've got a heart full of joy!

THINGS TO DO

- ○ Start thanking God for one new thing each day. You could even keep a "journal of joy"—find a pretty notebook and write in it all the things you're praising God for.

- ○ Share your joy journey with someone else. You can share your "thankful thing" with her each day.

- ○ Memorize a verse about praise.

- ○ Sing, dance, cheer! Celebrate God's good gifts!

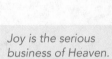

THINGS TO REMEMBER

Let us offer through Jesus a continual sacrifice of praise to God, proclaiming our allegiance to his name.
HEBREWS 13:15

I will exalt you, my God and King, and praise your name forever and ever.
PSALM 145:1

Praise the LORD!
Let all that I am praise the LORD.
I will praise the LORD as long as I live.
I will sing praises to my God with my dying breath. **PSALM 146:1-2**

"Blessings on the King who comes in the name of the LORD! Peace in heaven, and glory in highest heaven!"
But some of the Pharisees among the crowd said, "Teacher, rebuke your followers for saying things like that!" He replied, "If they kept quiet, the stones along the road would burst into cheers!" **LUKE 19:38-40**

We praise God for the glorious grace he has poured out on us who belong to his dear Son.
EPHESIANS 1:6

Joy is the serious business of Heaven.
C. S. LEWIS

Joy does not simply happen to us. We have to choose joy and keep choosing it every day.
HENRI NOUWEN

There is not one blade of grass, there is no color in this world that is not intended to make us rejoice.
JOHN CALVIN

What Are You Bragging About?

He gives grace generously. As the Scriptures say,

"God opposes the proud but gives grace to the humble."

JAMES 4:6

"BELLA THE BRAGGER STRIKES AGAIN!" Krista mumbled to her friends as Bella loudly described her new, very expensive sweater. Of course no one would call her that to her face. But Bella's friends were very tired of hearing her talk about how beautiful she was, how smart she was, how talented she was, how popular she was, how much money she had, and on and on and on. Whatever the topic of conversation, Bella could turn it into a brag. For example, Krista once said, "I really like tennis. I think I could be a good player if I—"

Yep, Bella interrupted with, "Oh, I'm an expert tennis player. I have my own pro. She's taught me a lot, and I'm about ready to become a pro myself at the club now." Whew.

One time someone even said, "Don't you think anyone else is good at stuff? Do you think we always want to hear about you?" But Bella didn't even seem to pay attention. She went right on talking about herself. She didn't notice how disgusted the other girls were or how they started avoiding her.

Bella is full of pride. That's obvious, right? But seriously, what does she have to be proud of? She must not understand that everything she has—any ability or talent or beauty or even money—is a gift from God. She had nothing to do with it.

Do you get it? Everything you have and everything you are is given to you by God. There is no place for pride, 'cause you had nothing to do with it. Besides, as this verse in James says, God doesn't look too favorably on pride. Be humble. Give all praise and glory to God. It's all about him.

CHECKUP TIME

On a scale of 1 to 5, where do you rank on the humility vs. pride spectrum?

1 = never
2 = not very often
3 = sometimes
4 = most of the time
5 = always

I compliment others on their skills and talents.

    1 2 3 4 5

I know I have nothing to brag about.

    1 2 3 4 5

I like seeing others succeed.

    1 2 3 4 5

I thank God for all he has given me.

    1 2 3 4 5

Humility comes easily to me.

    1 2 3 4 5

KEY

MOSTLY 1s Know what you're really good at? Being prideful. Ask God to help you adjust the way you see yourself.

MOSTLY 2s You are pretty impressed with yourself, aren't you? Try focusing on others for a change—compliment someone else today!

MOSTLY 3s It's good to have a healthy self-esteem, but remember that all you have and are comes from God. Ask him to help you catch yourself when you're about to brag and thank him instead.

MOSTLY 4s Pretty good! You are understanding God's role in your life.

MOSTLY 5s Great job! All praise to God for his gifts!

THINGS TO DO

○ Write a prayer of thanks to God for the talents and abilities he has given you.

○ Compliment another person for something each day.

○ Memorize a verse, such as James 4:6, that will remind you to be humble.

○ Try to go an entire day without talking about yourself.

THINGS TO REMEMBER

You who are younger must accept the authority of the elders. And all of you, dress yourselves in humility as you relate to one another, for "God opposes the proud but gives grace to the humble." **1 PETER 5:5**

Anyone who becomes as humble as this little child is the greatest in the Kingdom of Heaven. **MATTHEW 18:4**

Haughtiness goes before destruction; humility precedes honor. **PROVERBS 18:12**

Those who exalt themselves will be humbled, and those who humble themselves will be exalted. **MATTHEW 23:12**

The high and lofty one who lives in eternity, the Holy One, says this: "I live in the high and holy place with those whose spirits are contrite and humble. I restore the crushed spirit of the humble and revive the courage of those with repentant hearts." **ISAIAH 57:15**

What kills the skunk is the publicity it gives itself.
ABRAHAM LINCOLN

A man wrapped up in himself makes a very small bundle.
BENJAMIN FRANKLIN

Humility is to make a right estimate of one's self.
CHARLES HADDON SPURGEON

Keeping Score

[Love] is not irritable, and it keeps no record of being wronged.
1 CORINTHIANS 13:5

SUSIE KEEPS A JOURNAL, a private book that she hides away in her room. She doesn't write in it every day. But when she has something important to say, she grabs her journal and scribbles it down. Here's an example of some things Susie has written:

1. Today Linda was mean to me. It's the third time this week!
2. Mara wouldn't let me play with her group on the playground again.
3. Ryan was showing off in class again today.

Susie's journal is filled with things about people who have made her angry. It's got a lot of things written in it. That's because Susie is not easy to get along with, and she has a quick temper. When she gets angry, she doesn't forget who made her mad and why—ever.

Susie should study 1 Corinthians 13, especially verse 5, and learn what it means to love others. Maybe Susie is a little too touchy and gets angry too easily. Maybe she always wants her own way, and she needs to think about others more often. The truth is, most of the time people do not mean to hurt her feelings or make her angry, so she should just forgive them and move on—definitely *not* keep a record!

Loving others God's way means trying not to be crabby and forgiving others when they hurt you. Love doesn't keep score. It forgives and forgets.

CHECKUP TIME

On a scale of 1 to 5, how forgiving are you?

1 = never
2 = not very often
3 = sometimes
4 = most of the time
5 = always

When someone hurts me, I forgive easily.

1   2   3   4   5

I can forgive *and* forget; I am able to move on and not relive the memory over and over.

1   2   3   4   5

I choose not to hold grudges.

1   2   3   4   5

It's important to me that others forgive me.

1   2   3   4   5

I'm considerate of others and try not to hurt anyone.

1   2   3   4   5

KEY

MOSTLY 1s Uh-oh. Do you have a journal like Susie's? Ask God to help you get rid of your scorecard.

MOSTLY 2s Think about how often your friends need to forgive you. Would you want them to be as unforgiving as you are?

MOSTLY 3s Fair, but you can do better. Is there a past wrong you're having trouble forgiving completely? Ask God for his help.

MOSTLY 4s You're getting the idea. Keep working on growing in love and forgiveness.

MOSTLY 5s Way to go! You're loving others the way God teaches!

THINGS TO DO

○ Write a note to someone you need to forgive. Tell that person that you forgive him or her and you're sorry for holding a grudge.

○ Do you find yourself still getting upset about something you've already decided to forgive? Ask God to help you move on completely. Every time the painful memory comes to mind, pray for God to bless the person who hurt you.

○ Memorize a verse about forgiving and loving.

○ Thank God for his forgiveness.

THINGS TO REMEMBER

Dear friends, never take revenge. Leave that to the righteous anger of God. For the Scriptures say,

"I will take revenge;
I will pay them back,"
says the LORD. **ROMANS 12:19**

If you forgive those who sin against you, your heavenly Father will forgive you. But if you refuse to forgive others, your Father will not forgive your sins. **MATTHEW 6:14-15**

Watch yourselves! If another believer sins, rebuke that person; then if there is repentance, forgive. Even if that person wrongs you seven times a day and each time turns again and asks forgiveness, you must forgive. **LUKE 17:3-4**

Do not judge others, and you will not be judged. Do not condemn others, or it will all come back against you. Forgive others, and you will be forgiven. **LUKE 6:37**

Be kind to each other, tenderhearted, forgiving one another, just as God through Christ has forgiven you. **EPHESIANS 4:32**

Write injuries in sand, kindnesses in marble.
FRENCH PROVERB

God pardons like a mother, who kisses the offense into everlasting forgiveness.
HENRY WARD BEECHER

He that cannot forgive others, breaks the bridge over which he himself must pass if he would ever reach heaven; for everyone has need to be forgiven.
GEORGE HERBERT

Put It into Action

Don't just listen to God's word. You must do what it says. Otherwise, you are only fooling yourselves.
JAMES 1:22

COURTNEY HAS A FANTASTIC MEMORY. Seriously. She can read something once or twice and it is stuck in her mind. It's quite a gift. She uses her fantastic memory to win all sorts of contests, like memorizing Bible verses in her church club program. Courtney holds the record for most verses memorized—word for word!

Club meets tonight, and the theme for the night is loving others. Courtney has memorized twenty verses about love. She just knows she will win. Sure enough, Courtney quotes all twenty verses about loving others, word for word, and wins the contest. Afterward, Laney, the second-place winner, comes over to congratulate Courtney. But instead of being loving and friendly, Courtney says, "Ha! You didn't have a chance against me. Second place is really just first-place loser, you know!"

Ouch. Courtney has learned all those Bible verses about love, but she doesn't put what they say into action. She learns what the Bible says but doesn't *do* what it says. What's the point of learning it then?

It's good to read the Bible. It's good to memorize it. But the most important thing is to put the words of the Bible into action—make them a part of your life. That shows that you really do want to live for God and you want the words of the Bible to change you.

On a scale of 1 to 5, how well are you living out biblical teaching?

1 = never
2 = not very often
3 = sometimes
4 = most of the time
5 = always

When I learn a verse, I consciously try to put it into action in my life.

1   2   3   4   5

I believe it's important to live the way the Bible teaches.

1   2   3   4   5

I don't think God is satisfied if I just learn verses without putting them into practice.

1   2   3   4   5

I want to be an example of godly living for others to see.

1   2   3   4   5

I care that I'm pleasing God by how I live.

1   2   3   4   5

KEY

MOSTLY 1s Well, you aren't taking living for God very seriously. Ask him to change your attitude.

MOSTLY 2s You know that hearing about God and learning verses are important, but you need to do more. Ask God to help you live out what you're learning.

MOSTLY 3s Not bad, but you can do better. Every time you learn a Bible verse, think about how you can apply it to your life.

MOSTLY 4s Great—it's not always easy to obey what the Bible teaches, but you're working on it. Keep going!

MOSTLY 5s You got it! Learn and live what the Bible teaches!

THINGS TO DO

○ Choose one command from the Bible, and for one week, work on making it a part of your life.

○ Learn three or four verses on the same topic, such as loving others, being kind, or spending time each day talking to God. Then put them into practice.

○ Ask God's forgiveness for not always taking his Word seriously.

○ Thank God for his Word and the help it gives in knowing how to live for him.

THINGS TO REMEMBER

Fix your thoughts on what is true, and honorable, and right, and pure, and lovely, and admirable. Think about things that are excellent and worthy of praise.
PHILIPPIANS 4:8

All Scripture is inspired by God and is useful to teach us what is true and to make us realize what is wrong in our lives. It corrects us when we are wrong and teaches us to do what is right. **2 TIMOTHY 3:16**

Your word is a lamp to guide my feet and a light for my path. **PSALM 119:105**

Faith comes from hearing, that is, hearing the Good News about Christ. **ROMANS 10:17**

The word of God is alive and powerful. It is sharper than the sharpest two-edged sword, cutting between soul and spirit, between joint and marrow. It exposes our innermost thoughts and desires. **HEBREWS 4:12**

God is not silent, has never been silent. It is the nature of God to speak. The second person of the Holy Trinity is called the Word.
A. W. TOZER

One act of obedience is better than one hundred sermons.
DIETRICH BONHOEFFER

Maturity comes from obedience, not necessarily from age.
LEONARD RAVENHILL

Wendy the Whiner

"I DON'T WANT TO CLEAN MY ROOM."

"Why do I have to eat broccoli?"

"I don't like doing book reports."

"Sari's chore is easier than mine."

As you can see, Wendy is a champion whiner. No matter what's going on, she finds something to complain about. She complains so much that now she has a reputation among her friends and family, and she has earned the nickname "Wendy the Whiner."

Wendy's mom dreads Wendy opening her mouth because she knows that every other word Wendy speaks is going to be negative. She argues rather than obeys. She complains about almost everything. She is just no fun to be around. Wendy mostly thinks about herself, not about helping others or cooperating. She doesn't care about getting along with others. She doesn't care about being part of a family or a team.

Are you a whiner? Loving others is one of the most important lessons in the Bible, but it's hard to be loving when you're complaining and whining about everything that happens. For sure, there are things that are not fun, things that wouldn't be your first choice of how to

spend your time. People who are obeying God do those hard jobs without complaining, because they prioritize getting along with others and doing things that help everyone. These people are known for being helpful, kind, and cooperative. Loving means putting yourself in second place so that others can be in first place. That's acting like Jesus. When you do that, you won't complain and whine all the time, because you care about how others feel. If Wendy would live this way, she could change her nickname from Wendy the Whiner to Wendy the Winner.

On a scale of 1 to 5, how much of a whiner are you?

1 = never
2 = not very often
3 = sometimes
4 = most of the time
5 = always

I do whatever my mom or dad tell me to do—no whining.

1   2   3   4   5

I am okay with not getting my way.

1   2   3   4   5

I'll do any job I'm given.

1   2   3   4   5

I care about having a reputation as a loving person.

1   2   3   4   5

I care what God thinks about me.

1   2   3   4   5

KEY

MOSTLY 1s Yikes! You're a champion whiner. Ask God to help you stop yourself when you feel tempted to complain.

MOSTLY 2s You need to do some serious work. Pray for God to change your heart so that you care more about others' feelings.

MOSTLY 3s Half-time whiner is still too much! With God's help, you can do better than that.

MOSTLY 4s Not bad! Keep working on that positive attitude! You're almost there.

MOSTLY 5s Congratulations! You are no whiner. You are a cooperator!

THINGS TO DO

- ○ If you've been a whiner, you may need to apologize to some people for how you've spoken to or treated them. Choose one person and apologize today.

- ○ Volunteer to do one of the jobs you usually complain about.

- ○ Ask God to help you control your whining and complaining.

- ○ Ask a parent to help you remember not to whine.

THINGS TO REMEMBER

Don't grumble about each other, brothers and sisters, or you will be judged. For look—the Judge is standing at the door! **JAMES 5:9**

I have learned how to be content with whatever I have. **PHILIPPIANS 4:11**

Since God chose you to be the holy people he loves, you must clothe yourselves with tenderhearted mercy, kindness, humility, gentleness, and patience. **COLOSSIANS 3:12**

Don't use foul or abusive language. Let everything you say be good and helpful, so that your words will be an encouragement to those who hear them. **EPHESIANS 4:29**

Your kindness will reward you, but your cruelty will destroy you. **PROVERBS 11:17**

Ultimately, all our complaints are directed against God.
WOODROW KROLL

What you're supposed to do when you don't like a thing is change it. If you can't change it, change the way you think about it. Don't complain.
MAYA ANGELOU

Don't complain, just work harder.
RANDY PAUSCH

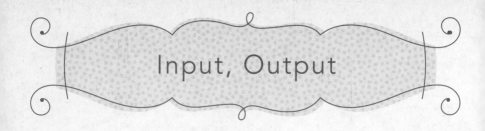

Input, Output

Fix your thoughts on what is true, and honorable, and right, and pure, and lovely, and admirable. Think about things that are excellent and worthy of praise.

PHILIPPIANS 4:8

TALLIE HAD SOME PRETTY PROBLEMATIC thoughts sometimes. She thought about what it might feel like to hit her little brother. She thought about ways she could take something that didn't belong to her. She thought about lies she could make up and tell others about a girl she didn't like. Tallie's mind was filled with mean, ugly, selfish, unkind thoughts. Not good. The more Tallie let the ugly, unkind thoughts roll around in her mind, the more ugly, unkind actions began to leak out into the way she behaved.

Pretty soon, instead of just thinking about hitting her brother, she was smacking him about once a day. One afternoon she was at a friend's house and thought about taking a pretty pink bracelet that belonged to her friend. Before she knew it, that bracelet was in her pocket! See, letting her thoughts run in a bad direction made her actions become hurtful to others. That's why God warns people to be careful what they think about.

Do you ever let your thoughts wander into places they shouldn't go? Do you let sinful thoughts play around in your mind? Be careful with that—what you put into your mind will eventually come out in your actions. A child of God should keep her thoughts on ways to be kind, ways to honor God, ways to show his love to others. Those thoughts will come out in actions that will please God and show others his love.

CHECKUP TIME

On a scale of 1 to 5, how do you rate your ability to keep your mind on track?

1 = never
2 = not very often
3 = sometimes
4 = most of the time
5 = always

When I have a bad thought, I chase it out of my mind.

    1   2   3   4   5

I try to keep pleasant, helpful thoughts in my mind.

    1   2   3   4   5

I know that bad thoughts don't result in good actions.

    1   2   3   4   5

I care about showing God's love through my actions.

    1   2   3   4   5

Good, pleasant thoughts are the first things to come into my mind.

    1   2   3   4   5

KEY

MOSTLY 1s Whoa, you need some serious help with those thoughts! Try to do at least one of the action steps on the next page every day this week.

MOSTLY 2s You need to get better control of your thoughts. Ask God to help you identify where your sinful thoughts might be coming from and to help you remove those things from your life.

MOSTLY 3s Don't let bad thoughts get comfy in your mind. Focus on replacing them with good ones.

MOSTLY 4s Not too bad! Keep thinking about what is good.

MOSTLY 5s Congratulations! You are honoring God in your thoughts!

THINGS TO DO

- ⭕ Make a list of where your negative thoughts could be coming from. Are you reading books, listening to music, or watching TV shows that promote sinful thinking or behavior?

- ⭕ Ask someone you trust to help you keep good thoughts in your mind, or to help you get rid of the sources of your bad thoughts.

- ⭕ Ask for God's help in controlling your thoughts.

- ⭕ Memorize a verse about kindness and love, and say it each time you have a negative thought.

THINGS TO REMEMBER

Those who are dominated by the sinful nature think about sinful things, but those who are controlled by the Holy Spirit think about things that please the Spirit. So letting your sinful nature control your mind leads to death. But letting the Spirit control your mind leads to life and peace. ROMANS 8:5-6

I, the LORD, search all hearts and examine secret motives. I give all people their due rewards, according to what their actions deserve. JEREMIAH 17:10

Whenever we have the opportunity, we should do good to everyone—especially to those in the family of faith. GALATIANS 6:10

Dear children, let's not merely say that we love each other; let us show the truth by our actions. 1 JOHN 3:18

Anyone who does not love does not know God, for God is love. 1 JOHN 4:8

Do all the good you can. By all the means you can. In all the ways you can. In all the places you can. At all the times you can. To all the people you can. As long as ever you can.
JOHN WESLEY

Sow a thought, reap an act; sow an act, reap a habit; sow a habit, reap a character; sow a character, reap a destiny.
UNKNOWN

The world we have created is a product of our thinking; it cannot be changed without changing our thinking.
ALBERT EINSTEIN

Sleep Tight

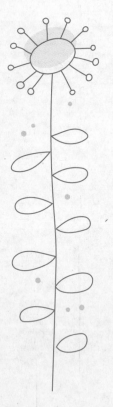

In peace I will lie down and sleep, for you alone, O LORD, will keep me safe.

PSALM 4:8

LISA COULDN'T SLEEP. She tossed and turned. She kicked her covers off, then right away pulled them back up. She fluffed her pillow. She got up for a drink of water. She turned the light on. The problem was . . . Lisa was scared. A house down the street had been robbed a few nights ago, and that terrified Lisa. She could not get past the fear that the same thing might happen at her house. She thought every noise was someone rattling a window. She thought every shadow was someone in her room. Lisa was letting her fears get the best of her. Her thoughts raced all night—and not in a good direction.

After a couple of nights with no sleep, Lisa told her parents about her fear. She should have done that right away! Her parents comforted her and then sat right down and prayed with her. They asked God to remind her that he was watching out for her. They prayed for help in trusting him. It helped Lisa to remember that God is always with her—both night and day.

Do you feel scared sometimes? Does your fear ever keep you awake? Maybe you need a reminder that God is always with you, too. It's a fact that scary things happen, but nothing happens to you that surprises God. He is right beside you, no matter what is happening. So when you feel scared, just ask him to help you remember that he is with you. Ask him to help you feel peaceful because you trust in him.

CHECKUP TIME

On a scale of 1 to 5, how much do you trust God when you're afraid?

1 = never
2 = not very often
3 = sometimes
4 = most of the time
5 = always

When I'm scared, the first thing I do is pray.

    1   2   3   4   5

When I have fearful thoughts, I tell myself that God is in control and think of positive things.

    1   2   3   4   5

I know I'm not alone because God is *always* with me.

    1   2   3   4   5

When I'm fearful, I tell my parents what's bothering me.

    1   2   3   4   5

When I pray about my fears, I feel better.

    1   2   3   4   5

KEY

MOSTLY 1s Poor thing, you must not get much sleep! Tell someone you trust about your fears.

MOSTLY 2s You need help getting your thoughts under control. Pick at least two of the action steps on the next page and commit to doing them this week.

MOSTLY 3s If you believe God is always with you, you don't have to feel scared even some of the time! Ask God to help your trust grow.

MOSTLY 4s You are doing a pretty good job at trusting God to take care of things. Keep looking to him for help.

MOSTLY 5s Way to go! You're trusting God to be with you and take care of you.

THINGS TO DO

○ Memorize a few verses to remind you that God is always with you.

○ Read a Bible story that tells how God protected his people.

○ Ask for God's help in trusting his presence and care.

○ Tell a trusted adult of your fear. Ask that adult to pray with you and for you.

THINGS TO REMEMBER

Be strong and courageous! Do not be afraid and do not panic before them. For the LORD your God will personally go ahead of you. He will neither fail you nor abandon you. **DEUTERONOMY 31:6**

Be strong and courageous! Do not be afraid or discouraged. For the LORD your God is with you wherever you go. **JOSHUA 1:9**

When I am afraid,
I will put my trust in you.
I praise God for what he has promised.
I trust in God, so why should I be afraid?
What can mere mortals do to me?
PSALM 56:3-4

I hold you by your right hand—
I, the LORD your God.
And I say to you,
"Don't be afraid. I am here to help you."
ISAIAH 41:13

God has not given us a spirit of fear and timidity, but of power, love, and self-discipline.
2 TIMOTHY 1:7

The only thing we have to fear is fear itself—nameless, unreasoning, unjustified terror which paralyzes needed efforts to convert retreat into advance.
FRANKLIN DELANO ROOSEVELT

Feed your fears, and your faith will starve. Feed your faith, and your fears will.
MAX LUCADO

Worry is a cycle of inefficient thoughts whirling around a center of fear.
CORRIE TEN BOOM

Quick Tempered

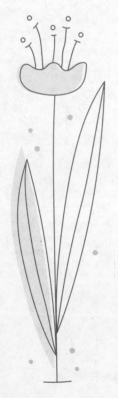

KARA WAS SHAKING IN HER BOOTS. She had to tell her sister, Macy, that she had accidentally broken Macy's favorite necklace. Everyone knew that Macy had a terrible temper, and that's why Kara was so nervous. The thing was, the break was an accident, and it was partially Macy's fault. Macy had left the necklace on the floor in the hallway, and Kara had stepped on it and broken it. But Kara knew that Macy wouldn't listen to any explanation. Her temper was like a volcano exploding. Kara had to be careful. "Ummm, Macy, can I, uhh, tell you something?" she asked softly.

"What did you do now?" Macy snapped.

"It was totally an accident, but your silver cross necklace sort of got broken," Kara almost whispered. "I'm really sor—"

Macy exploded before Kara could say another word. "You always break my stuff! Stay out of my room. Don't touch another thing of mine—I mean it!" she shouted. That was just the beginning. The harder Kara tried to explain, the louder Macy yelled. It was hopeless.

Macy does not understand the message of James 1:19. She isn't quick to listen—she doesn't even let Kara explain what happened. She isn't slow to speak—she starts shouting before she hears the whole story. She isn't slow to get angry—in fact, she is very quick to get angry. What does this do? It makes Kara feel terrible. It gives Macy the reputation of having a terrible temper. It damages the relationship between them. That's why God says to be slow at getting angry. It gives peace a chance.

So how are you at staying quiet when you want to get angry? Are you a good listener? Do you give others the benefit of the doubt? Are you good at keeping the peace?

CHECKUP TIME

On a scale of 1 to 5, how slow to anger are you?

1 = never
2 = not very often
3 = sometimes
4 = most of the time
5 = always

When things happen, I give others a chance to explain.

1   2   3   4   5

Even when I'm upset I speak kindly and with respect.

1   2   3   4   5

I show my love for God by not losing my temper.

1   2   3   4   5

Counting to ten before speaking works for me!

1   2   3   4   5

I want to hear the whole story before I speak.

1   2   3   4   5

KEY

MOSTLY 1s Yikes! Have you noticed people steering clear of you? Ask God to help you control your anger. Then ask a trusted adult to help you come up with a plan.

MOSTLY 2s You must feel like your temper is always just about to explode. God doesn't want that for you. Tell him that you want things to be different, starting today.

MOSTLY 3s You can do better than that. Pray that God will help you remember to treat others the way you want to be treated.

MOSTLY 4s Pretty good, but you can probably do even better! Don't give up until that temper is completely under control.

MOSTLY 5s Congratulations—you have learned that relationships are more important than winning a battle!

THINGS TO DO

- ○ Ask a friend or an adult to hold you accountable for keeping your temper under control.

- ○ Ask God to help you slow down and give people chances to explain.

- ○ Try counting to ten before you spout off in anger.

- ○ Before you get upset, remind yourself of how many times you do things that upset your friends or family.

THINGS TO REMEMBER

Don't use foul or abusive language. Let everything you say be good and helpful, so that your words will be an encouragement to those who hear them.
EPHESIANS 4:29

An angry person starts fights;
a hot-tempered person commits all kinds of sin. **PROVERBS 29:22**

Control your temper,
for anger labels you a fool.
ECCLESIASTES 7:9

People with understanding control their anger;
a hot temper shows great foolishness.
PROVERBS 14:29

God blesses those who work for peace,
for they will be called the children of God.
MATTHEW 5:9

God's definition of what matters is pretty straightforward. He measures our lives by how we love.
FRANCIS CHAN

You can either practice being right or practice being kind.
UNKNOWN

It's easier to leave angry words unspoken than to mend a heart those words have broken.
UNKNOWN

Put Your Money Where Your Mouth Is

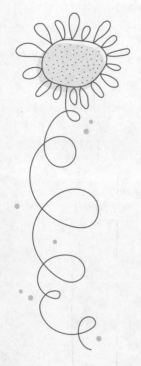

If someone has enough money to live well and sees a brother or sister in need but shows no compassion—how can God's love be in that person?

1 JOHN 3:17

SWANTI AND HER FRIENDS love pretty things like clothes and jewelry and shoes. Their favorite thing to do is go shopping. One of their moms takes the whole group to the mall and hangs out there while they shop. They have so much fun! They can easily spend the whole day there. Swanti's family isn't rich, but they are comfortable. She gets a decent allowance and earns more money by doing special jobs for neighbors. Swanti saves up her money then buys the prettiest things she can find. She enjoys dressing nice and having the latest stuff. She kind of sets the standard for everyone else.

But lately something has been bothering Swanti. "Hey, guys, have you seen the reports about all the people who have had to leave their homes and everything they own because of war and fighting in their countries? It's really sad. I mean, some of them are kids like us. They don't have fancy clothes. In fact, they may have only one thing to wear. Sometimes they don't even have food to eat."

"Yeah, that is bad. Hey, do you want to try that store that just opened? We should check it out," Swanti's friend Taylor said. She didn't really care about the serious things other people were facing. Swanti did, though. She cared enough about the problems of others that she did what she could—she gave some of her own money, money she would have enjoyed using for shopping. But Swanti decided that helping others was more important to her than shopping. She gave because she loves Jesus, and that's what he would do!

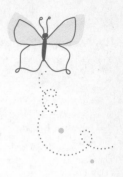

It's easy to *say* that you care about the difficult things other people have to deal with. But if you put actions with those words, then it shows that you truly do care. Do you?

CHECKUP TIME

On a scale of 1 to 5, how compassionate are you?

1 = never
2 = not very often
3 = sometimes
4 = most of the time
5 = always

I pay attention to the problems people around the world are dealing with.

1   2   3   4   5

I believe I have to do more than pray for others.

1   2   3   4   5

I feel bad when others are suffering.

1   2   3   4   5

I'd give up something I want in order to help others.

1   2   3   4   5

Showing God's love in practical ways is important to me.

1   2   3   4   5

KEY

MOSTLY 1s Whoa. Do you have a heart or a stone? Ask God to soften your heart toward the needs of others.

MOSTLY 2s You are a little too focused on yourself. Be on the lookout today for ways you can show love to someone else.

MOSTLY 3s Sometimes you're sensitive to what other people need, but your heart still gets distracted by your own desires. Pray that God will make your heart more like his.

MOSTLY 4s You do care for others. Keep looking for ways to demonstrate God's love.

MOSTLY 5s Bless you for your compassionate and generous heart!

THINGS TO DO

- ◯ Choose a cause or situation that grabs your heart and find out how you can help.

- ◯ Make a plan for helping someone else, either through giving money or time.

- ◯ Organize a way for others to join you in working for a good cause.

- ◯ Ask God to show you the best places to put your helping hand.

THINGS TO REMEMBER

You must be compassionate, just as your Father is compassionate.
LUKE 6:36

Share each other's burdens, and in this way obey the law of Christ. **GALATIANS 6:2**

Since God chose you to be the holy people he loves, you must clothe yourselves with tenderhearted mercy, kindness, humility, gentleness, and patience. **COLOSSIANS 3:12**

If you help the poor, you are lending to the LORD—
and he will repay you!
PROVERBS 19:17

Be happy with those who are happy, and weep with those who weep. **ROMANS 12:15**

To keep the Golden Rule we must put ourselves in other people's places, but to do that consists in and depends upon picturing ourselves in their places.
HARRY EMERSON FOSDICK

My mission in life is not merely to survive, but to thrive; and to do so with some passion, some compassion, some humor, and some style.
MAYA ANGELOU

No one has ever become poor by giving.
ANNE FRANK

The Real Problem

Smooth words may hide a wicked heart, just as a pretty glaze covers a clay pot.
PROVERBS 26:23

"HEY, COOL JEANS. You look really good in them," Rochelle said.

"Um, yeah, thanks," Elizabeth answered. She walked away shaking her head. She didn't believe much of what Rochelle said. Elizabeth and her friends knew that Rochelle would say nice, sugary-sweet things to their faces, but behind their backs she said mean and negative things. Like at that moment, Elizabeth thought Rochelle was probably telling someone how Elizabeth's new jeans made her look fat or how they looked cheap or how Elizabeth didn't have any idea what looks good.

Sure, Rochelle says nice things, but underneath those words are unkind, judgmental opinions—and her friends have come to know that. They have each been with her when she has said things such as, "Did you *see* Ciara's hair? She totally looks geeky." But then they hear her tell Ciara, "Awesome new haircut, girl. Lookin' good." Yeah, right.

Or she might say, "Don't worry that you only got a B on the test. I know you're super smart." But to others she says, "Whoa, what a loser she is. I'm guessing she has trouble spelling her own name!"

Does Rochelle really think she is fooling

anyone? Maybe she doesn't even realize that her sugary-sweet words are an
attempt to hide a mean-spirited heart.
Rochelle needs to forget the showy words
and just get her heart cleaned up. Then
the words she speaks will be sincere and
not cover-ups.

You see, the truth is that sweet words
turn sour when people know that you don't
mean them. The real problem is a heart
that is angry and critical, which might be
that way because it is hurting. Ask God to
help you take care of what's going on in
your heart, and then you will be able to
speak kindly—and honestly—to others.

On a scale of 1 to 5, how honest are your words?

1 = never
2 = not very often
3 = sometimes
4 = most of the time
5 = always

I think about how my words make others feel.

1   2   3   4   5

I believe that honesty is the best policy.

1   2   3   4   5

I ask God to help me speak honestly and kindly.

1   2   3   4   5

I care whether my friends believe what I say.

1   2   3   4   5

Deep in my heart I am happy and secure.

1   2   3   4   5

KEY

MOSTLY 1s It's doubtful that anyone believes what you say anymore. But don't be discouraged—God can still turn you around.

MOSTLY 2s Sounds like you need to deal with some junk in your heart. Ask God to show you where your insincere or unkind attitudes are coming from.

MOSTLY 3s You've started your journey, but you still have a ways to go. Keep working with God on that heart of yours!

MOSTLY 4s You usually speak honestly and kindly. Keep up the good work!

MOSTLY 5s Good for you—your kind, honest words reflect a kind, honest heart!

THINGS TO DO

- ○ Ask a trusted friend whether she believes the things you say.

- ○ Ask a parent or another adult to hold you accountable for things you say.

- ○ Stop and think about how you really feel about others. Do you need to work on your own heart health?

- ○ Ask God to help you get your heart healthy and keep it that way.

THINGS TO REMEMBER

An honest answer
is like a kiss of friendship.
PROVERBS 24:26

If you claim to be religious but don't control your tongue, you are fooling yourself, and your religion is worthless. **JAMES 1:26**

Let your conversation be gracious and attractive so that you will have the right response for everyone. **COLOSSIANS 4:6**

Take control of what I say, O LORD, and guard my lips. **PSALM 141:3**

Timely advice is lovely,
like golden apples in a silver basket.
PROVERBS 25:11

Friends, if we be honest with ourselves, we shall be honest with each other.
GEORGE MACDONALD

Safety and happiness can only come from individuals, classes, and nations being honest and fair and kind to each other.
C. S. LEWIS

An honest heart is open to the Word.
A. W. PINK

Look Around

"SLEEPOVER AT MY HOUSE Friday night! You're all invited, and we are gonna have *so much fun!*" Ashlee shouted. Her five friends cheered and started talking about doing their nails and watching movies and all the other fun things they were going to do. It sounded awesome! At least it sounded awesome if you were invited. Rebecca wasn't. She was new to the school. She didn't have any friends. She was lonely. Rebecca watched Ashlee and her friends every day and just wished that she could be a part of their little group. They seemed like nice girls, but to them, Rebecca was invisible. None of them had ever even said hi to her.

Rebecca didn't live far from Ashlee. She had passed Ashlee's house several times and had seen the girls through the window. More than anything, Rebecca wished that one of them would say hello to her. She wished that one of them would take the time to get to know her. Rebecca just wanted a friend.

It's hard to be the new girl in school—or anywhere. Girls who already have a group of friends sometimes don't notice some- one who is lonely. It takes an intentional outlook—looking around to see girls who are often by themselves and then having the courage to go over and say hello.

A girl who is trying to live for God will make an effort to talk with newcomers. She will understand how lonely life can be with no friends.

Have you looked around lately? Are there new kids in your school, your neighborhood, your church? Have you tried to get to know them? Be the one to take the first step to welcome new people into your group.

CHECKUP TIME

On a scale of 1 to 5, how are you doing at noticing lonely people?

1 = never
2 = not very often
3 = sometimes
4 = most of the time
5 = always

I love talking to people I don't know.

    1   2   3   4   5

I bring my friends along to meet new people.

    1   2   3   4   5

I invite new girls to join my friends and me.

    1   2   3   4   5

Even if my friends don't like it, I bring along new people.

    1   2   3   4   5

I tell my friends it's important to be kind to others.

    1   2   3   4   5

KEY

MOSTLY 1s Hmm. You need to open your eyes and heart to others. Ask God to give you his love for the lonely.

MOSTLY 2s Can you think of someone who needs a friend right now? Commit to reaching out to that person this week.

MOSTLY 3s Sometimes you reach out, but other times you stay put in your comfort zone. Ask God to grow your compassion and courage.

MOSTLY 4s You're a generally friendly person—keep reaching out!

MOSTLY 5s Good for you. Your kindness and friendliness are an inspiration to others!

THINGS TO DO

○ Talk to one person today whom you don't know.

○ Ask someone new to sit with you and your friends at lunch.

○ Encourage your group to include someone new the next time you have a sleepover or do something else together.

○ Ask God to help you notice someone who is an outsider.

THINGS TO REMEMBER

Don't just pretend to love others. Really love them. Hate what is wrong. Hold tightly to what is good. **ROMANS 12:9**

Dear friends, let us continue to love one another, for love comes from God. Anyone who loves is a child of God and knows God.
1 JOHN 4:7

If I could speak all the languages of earth and of angels, but didn't love others, I would only be a noisy gong or a clanging cymbal.
1 CORINTHIANS 13:1

What good is it, dear brothers and sisters, if you say you have faith but don't show it by your actions? Can that kind of faith save anyone?
JAMES 2:14

[Jesus said,] "Now I am giving you a new commandment: Love each other. Just as I have loved you, you should love each other."
JOHN 13:34

Our love to God will be measured by our everyday fellowship with other people and the love it displays.
ANDREW MURRAY

Don't wait for people to be friendly. Show them how.
UNKNOWN

I believe that life is given us so that we may grow in love, and I believe that God is in me as the sun is in the color and fragrance of a flower.
HELEN KELLER

Just Remember

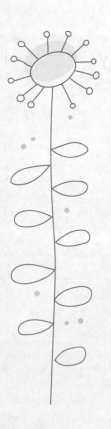

Give all your worries and cares to God, for he cares about you.

1 PETER 5:7

"I DON'T CARE IF THE SUN IS SHINING. I don't care if you are all going to the pool. I don't care if there is a pizza party tonight. Just leave me alone, okay? Leave me alone." Megan didn't shout this at her friends. She said it softly, as if her heart was breaking . . . because it was. Megan's mom and dad were splitting up. There had been a lot of yelling and even a little bit of throwing things. They had tried therapy, but that just seemed to make things worse. So now her dad had moved out, and Megan hadn't seen him for several weeks. Her mom wouldn't talk about him or about what was going to happen. Megan was pretty sure they would get divorced. But she couldn't even bring herself to say the word. She couldn't help wondering if there was something she could have done to fix things. It felt like there was nothing stable in her world anymore.

Megan's friends kept trying to cheer her up, but Megan couldn't think about anything except her family disintegrating.

There are no real winners in a divorce. It's even harder when there are kids who are left wondering what they did wrong or whether they could have stopped things. They miss the parent who has left, and they feel their loyalties stretched between the two. No fun.

If your parents have split up, just know that they both still love you. The one who left surely misses you a lot. Even though the broken family will no doubt always hurt, the pain will get better. The important thing to remember is that God cares more than you can imagine, because he loves you more than you can imagine.

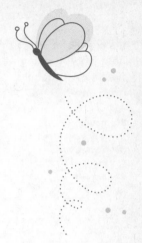

CHECKUP TIME

On a scale of 1 to 5, how are you doing at dealing with family problems?

1 = never
2 = not very often
3 = sometimes
4 = most of the time
5 = always

I know God cares, and that helps a lot.

   1   2   3   4   5

I know my parents' problems are not my fault.

   1   2   3   4   5

I pray for my mom and dad every day.

   1   2   3   4   5

I let my friends help me deal with things.

   1   2   3   4   5

I believe my parents love me.

   1   2   3   4   5

KEY

MOSTLY 1s Wow, you're really hurting, aren't you? Ask God to show you a trusted friend or adult who can help you.

MOSTLY 2s You're still struggling to believe in God's care. Keep talking to him, even if it doesn't feel like he's listening. He is.

MOSTLY 3s You're surviving, but things are still rough. It might help to talk with your parents.

MOSTLY 4s You are doing a pretty good job handling your emotions. But remember to ask for help when you need it.

MOSTLY 5s Leaning on God, you are making it through a tough situation.

THINGS TO DO

- ○ Talk to your parents, individually or together. Tell them how you're feeling. Don't be afraid of hurting their feelings or bothering them; it's true that they have their own problems, but they need to know how you feel too.

- ○ If you can't talk with your parents, talk with another trusted adult.

- ○ Pray—a lot. Ask God to comfort you and help you through these tough times.

- ○ Pick one of the verses in today's devotional and read it a few times a day until you've memorized it. Recite it to yourself whenever you feel overwhelmed by sadness.

THINGS TO REMEMBER

The very hairs on your head are all numbered. So don't be afraid; you are more valuable to God than a whole flock of sparrows. MATTHEW 10:30-31

My health may fail, and my spirit may grow weak, but God remains the strength of my heart; he is mine forever. PSALM 73:26

Do not be afraid or discouraged, for the LORD will personally go ahead of you. He will be with you; he will neither fail you nor abandon you. DEUTERONOMY 31:8

Even when I walk
through the darkest valley,
I will not be afraid,
for you are close beside me.
Your rod and your staff
protect and comfort me. PSALM 23:4

Now let your unfailing love comfort me, just as you promised me, your servant. PSALM 119:76

God loves each of us as if there were only one of us.
ST. AUGUSTINE

You are not what others think you are. You are what God knows you are.
SHANNON L. ALDER

There is no surprise more magical than the surprise of being loved. It is God's finger on man's shoulder.
CHARLES MORGAN

Saving the World

LAILA LOVES JESUS. She became a Christian when she was only six years old and has tried to obey Jesus and live for him ever since. She thinks it would be really awesome if everyone in the whole world became followers of Jesus. Laila and her family give money every month to some missionaries that their church supports. The work they do helps people around the world learn about God's love. Sometimes the missionaries come to Laila's church and tell about their work. They show pictures of the places they live and the people they work with. It's pretty cool.

I wonder if I could be a missionary someday, Laila thinks. But it's kind of scary to think about moving across the world, away from family. She's not sure she could do it.

Laila doesn't have to make that decision right now. She can pray for God's guidance and direction in her life, and he will show her how she can serve him as she grows up. But the cool thing is that she can share God's love right now—with her neighbors, her classmates, and anyone else she knows.

When Jesus said to go into all the world and preach the gospel, he knew that some people would cross oceans to be missionaries. Some people would be pastors at home. Some would just be regular people who share their love for Jesus with their friends and family. That's how "all the world" is covered.

What do you think about this command from Jesus? Do you think about people in your town, state, country, and around the world who have never even heard of God's love? Does that make you sad? Have you thought about what you can do to share God's message?

CHECKUP TIME

On a scale of 1 to 5, how seriously do you take Jesus' command?

1 = never
2 = not very often
3 = sometimes
4 = most of the time
5 = always

I think about people who have never had a chance to hear of God's love.

1   2   3   4   5

I think about how I can obey Jesus' command to tell others about him.

1   2   3   4   5

I pray for missionaries.

1   2   3   4   5

I am willing to tell others about Jesus.

1   2   3   4   5

I think Jesus' command is for everyone, not just pastors and missionaries.

1   2   3   4   5

KEY

MOSTLY 1s You do understand that those who don't know Jesus cannot go to heaven, right? Ask God to help you love people like he does—and to share his love with them.

MOSTLY 2s Remember that someone once told you about Jesus' love. Ask God for the opportunity to be that person for someone else.

MOSTLY 3s You care about telling others about Jesus, but other things sometimes get in the way. Pray that God will help you follow through.

MOSTLY 4s Good—you're understanding how serious this is. Keep letting Jesus' love shine through you!

MOSTLY 5s Hooray! You have a heart for all people to learn about Jesus!

THINGS TO DO

- ○ Think of one person you can begin to pray for and share your faith with.

- ○ Memorize Mark 16:15 so you don't forget Jesus' command.

- ○ Pray for missionaries every day.

- ○ Ask God to give you a passion that all people would get a chance to hear about his love.

THINGS TO REMEMBER

Go and make disciples of all the nations, baptizing them in the name of the Father and the Son and the Holy Spirit.
MATTHEW 28:19

[Jesus] said to his disciples, "The harvest is great, but the workers are few. So pray to the Lord who is in charge of the harvest; ask him to send more workers into his fields."
MATTHEW 9:37-38

I heard the Lord asking, "Whom should I send as a messenger to this people? Who will go for us?"
I said, "Here I am. Send me." **ISAIAH 6:8**

I am not ashamed of this Good News about Christ. It is the power of God at work, saving everyone who believes—the Jew first and also the Gentile. **ROMANS 1:16**

The wages of sin is death, but the free gift of God is eternal life through Christ Jesus our Lord. **ROMANS 6:23**

As soon as a man has found Christ, he begins to find others.
CHARLES HADDON SPURGEON

I would not give one moment of heaven for all the joy and riches of the world, even if it lasted for thousands and thousands of years.
MARTIN LUTHER

God keeps no half-way house. It's either heaven or hell for you and me.
BILLY SUNDAY

Gone, Not Forgotten

We put our hope in the LORD. He is our help and our shield.
PSALM 33:20

"HEY, LAURA, LET'S PUT UP the Christmas decorations," Tim said to his older sister. He was too little to do it by himself, but Laura just didn't want to.

"Tim, there isn't going to be any Christmas this year," Laura said. She went into her room and closed the door.

"Laura, please?" Tim stood outside her door, begging. She knew he didn't really understand why she didn't want to decorate. He was so little that the situation just went over his head.

How do I do this, God? Tell me, why did you think it would be a good idea for my mom to die? I'm just wondering, 'cause I don't think it was such a great idea. I miss her. A lot, Laura prayed silently.

It had been only two months since her mom died, and Laura's heart was still hurting more than she could explain to anyone. She missed her mom's laugh. She missed baking cookies with her. She missed singing silly songs and shopping and knitting lessons and, well . . . everything.

It was hard to think about anything being normal again—especially Christmas. Laura couldn't find the energy to celebrate, not even for Tim's sake.

Losing someone you love is so hard. It

hurts a lot, even if you know your loved one was a Christian and that you'll see him or her again in heaven someday. You still feel the loss and grief and hurt for right now. And it's okay to feel those things. You shouldn't try to push those feelings away, because they are part of the grief process. It's healthy to let them come out. But in your grieving, remember that God loves you and he cares that you're hurting so much. Tell him how you feel. Ask him to comfort you and remind you of the hope of heaven. He will help you. He wants to.

CHECKUP TIME

On a scale of 1 to 5, how do you handle grief?

1 = never
2 = not very often
3 = sometimes
4 = most of the time
5 = always

When I'm sad, I remember that God is still with me.

1   2   3   4   5

I tell someone how I'm feeling and accept their comfort.

1   2   3   4   5

I know God cares.

1   2   3   4   5

The promise of being with my loved one in heaven someday comforts me.

1   2   3   4   5

I know it's okay to cry.

1   2   3   4   5

KEY

MOSTLY 1s It sounds like you're having a really hard time. You need to ask a parent or another trustworthy adult for help.

MOSTLY 2s This is tough stuff. Talk to someone you trust about how you feel.

MOSTLY 3s You have your ups and downs. Keep asking God to comfort you.

MOSTLY 4s You're doing better. It takes time for such a deep wound to heal.

MOSTLY 5s Good. You're remembering that Jesus loves you and allowing him to help you with your grief.

THINGS TO DO

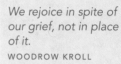

○ First, remember that it's okay to be sad. You lost someone you love.

○ Choose some comforting verses that really help you. Write them down and put them in places where you'll see them often.

○ Talk with someone who knew your loved one. Share memories.

○ Ask God to comfort you and give you good memories of your loved one.

THINGS TO REMEMBER

O Lord, you alone are my hope. I've trusted you, O LORD, from childhood. **PSALM 71:5**

God blesses those who mourn, for they will be comforted. **MATTHEW 5:4**

The LORD is good, a strong refuge when trouble comes. He is close to those who trust in him. **NAHUM 1:7**

The LORD is close to the brokenhearted; he rescues those whose spirits are crushed. **PSALM 34:18**

Give all your worries and cares to God, for he cares about you. **1 PETER 5:7**

We rejoice in spite of our grief, not in place of it.
WOODROW KROLL

God always gives His best to those who leave the choice with Him.
JIM ELLIOT

Jesus gives us hope because He keeps us company, has a vision, and knows the way we should go.
MAX LUCADO

Like a Blinking Light

Keep your servant from deliberate sins! Don't let them control me.

Then I will be free of guilt and innocent of great sin.

PSALM 19:13

KALLIE FELT LIKE HER BACKPACK had a flashing light inside, blinking off and on to call attention to itself. *I can't believe I did this. I can't believe it. What was I thinking?* Kallie thought as she hurried home. Here's what happened: Kallie's teacher sent her to the school office to deliver a folder. As she left it on the counter, Kallie noticed an iPod that someone had turned in to Lost and Found. She had always wanted an iPod. No one was looking, so Kallie swept it off the counter and into her backpack—smooth. No one saw a thing. She left the office and started home, but now it seemed like that stolen iPod was a blinking light in her backpack, telling everyone where it was.

Of course the iPod wasn't blinking. What Kallie was feeling was plain old guilt. Kallie wasn't in the habit of taking things that weren't hers. She knew that stealing was wrong. How was she going to explain this iPod to her parents? Would she have to make up a lie to cover the theft? What if it actually belonged to someone she knew? Whoa. No fun.

Every day you make choices to do right or do wrong. As your faith grows stronger and you learn to follow Christ, you will make more right choices than wrong ones. You know it's wrong to take something that doesn't belong to you, even if it's something you really want. Making one wrong choice requires more wrong behavior to try to cover up the first sin. Whew. Tiring. So what do you do? Simple—don't make wrong choices in the first place. But if you do, confess—both to the person you wronged and to God. Ask forgiveness, and strive to do better next time.

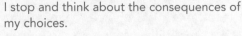

On a scale of 1 to 5, how carefully do you think about the choices you make?

1 = never
2 = not very often
3 = sometimes
4 = most of the time
5 = always

I stop and think about the consequences of my choices.

1   2   3   4   5

I avoid any decision that will cause me guilt later.

1   2   3   4   5

I know that others are often affected by my choices.

1   2   3   4   5

I care about obeying and honoring God with my choices.

1   2   3   4   5

I pay attention to what the Bible teaches as to how I should live.

1   2   3   4   5

KEY

MOSTLY 1s Yikes! Your habit of acting without considering the consequences is going to get you in big trouble someday, if it hasn't already. Ask God to help you think about your choices before you make them.

MOSTLY 2s Galatians 6:7 says, "You will always harvest what you plant." Talk to a friend or an adult you trust about what this means.

MOSTLY 3s You've learned a thing or two, but you're still struggling to make good choices consistently. Keep praying for God's help.

MOSTLY 4s Sounds like you usually stop and think about your choices. Remember to always seek God's guidance in your decisions.

MOSTLY 5s Congrats! You care about honoring God and others through the choices you make.

THINGS TO DO

○ Are you facing some big decisions? List the pros and cons of the choices you have. Pray and ask God to give you wisdom.

○ Think about the consequences that resulted from your last quick, bad choice. Was it worth it?

○ Memorize a verse about making good choices.

○ Ask God to stop you before making a bad choice by reminding you that you belong to him.

THINGS TO REMEMBER

If you refuse to serve the LORD, then choose today whom you will serve. Would you prefer the gods your ancestors served beyond the Euphrates? Or will it be the gods of the Amorites in whose land you now live? But as for me and my family, we will serve the LORD. **JOSHUA 24:15**

Show me the right path, O LORD;
point out the road for me to follow.
PSALM 25:4

[The Lord] renews my strength.
He guides me along right paths,
bringing honor to his name. **PSALM 23:3**

If you need wisdom, ask our generous God, and he will give it to you. He will not rebuke you for asking. **JAMES 1:5**

Come and listen to my counsel.
I'll share my heart with you
and make you wise. **PROVERBS 1:23**

The remarkable thing is we have a choice every day regarding the attitude we will embrace for that day.
CHUCK SWINDOLL

Every choice you make has an end result.
ZIG ZIGLAR

When the believer is faced with a decision regarding a questionable matter, he should never proceed unless he has complete peace about it. If there is nothing wrong with it, then God is able to give complete peace.
CURTIS HUTSON

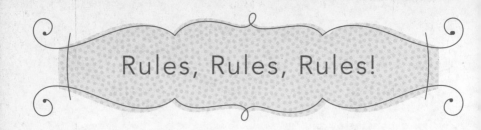

Rules, Rules, Rules!

My child, listen when your father corrects you. Don't neglect your mother's instruction.
PROVERBS 1:8

SHANA STOMPED UP THE STAIRS to her room and slammed the door. She felt that her parents treated her like a little kid. They had way too many rules. This time she had gotten in trouble for going to her friend Olivia's house when Shana's parents weren't home. Shana didn't see why it was such a big deal. Her parents knew Olivia and Olivia's parents. Shana had been to Olivia's house, like, a bazillion times. It's not like she could have asked her parents' permission to go, since Mom was driving her brother somewhere and Dad wasn't home from work. It's just that they had this dumb rule that she couldn't leave home until one of them was there to give permission.

When Mom got home, she went to Shana's room to ask her a question, and Shana wasn't there. Then Mom panicked. She told Shana that she had gone all over the house looking for her. Then she called Shana's friends until she found her.

Now Shana is grounded . . . for a long time. Her dad tried to explain why this rule is so important—for Shana's safety and so they know where she is all the time and blah, blah, blah. Shana just doesn't get it.

Shana doesn't understand that her parents just want her to be safe. She doesn't see that there's a reason parents make rules and a reason God says to obey those rules.

God says it's important to honor your parents and their rules. Rules teach you how to live with other people and treat them with respect.

Do you obey your parents? Do you honor the rules they make for you? Do you understand that rules are for your own good? Obey God by obeying your parents' rules and showing honor to them.

CHECKUP TIME

On a scale of 1 to 5, how are you doing at obeying your parents' rules?

1 = never
2 = not very often
3 = sometimes
4 = most of the time
5 = always

I keep the rules—even when Mom and Dad aren't around.

    1   2   3   4   5

I know my parents' rules are for my safety.

    1   2   3   4   5

I obey my parents because God says to.

    1   2   3   4   5

I obey without arguing.

    1   2   3   4   5

I believe obeying rules helps me learn to be a better person.

    1   2   3   4   5

KEY

MOSTLY 1s Yikes. You have lots of work to do! Ask God to help you change your attitude toward your parents.

MOSTLY 2s So . . . obeying isn't your strong point. Time to change that! Obeying your parents is one of the best ways to show your love for God.

MOSTLY 3s You're good at sticking to the rules when you feel like it. But what about when it means giving up something you really want to do? Ask God to help you obey even when it's hard.

MOSTLY 4s Not bad. But you can do even better. Remember that honoring your parents honors God.

MOSTLY 5s Good for you. You understand the importance of obeying rules and do your best to keep them.

THINGS TO DO

○ If your parents have rules you don't understand or don't agree with, ask to talk with them—respectfully!—about those rules.

○ Ask your parents what you must do to show them you can be trusted enough to have some rules lifted or changed.

○ Write out any particular rule you have trouble with so that you see it and are reminded to obey it.

○ The best way to get better at obeying? Ask God to help you, even when it's hard.

THINGS TO REMEMBER

Honor your father and mother. Then you will live a long, full life in the land the LORD your God is giving you. **EXODUS 20:12**

Children, obey your parents because you belong to the Lord, for this is the right thing to do. **EPHESIANS 6:1**

If you honor your father and mother, "things will go well for you, and you will have a long life on the earth." **EPHESIANS 6:3**

Children, always obey your parents, for this pleases the Lord. **COLOSSIANS 3:20**

Merely listening to the law doesn't make us right with God. It is obeying the law that makes us right in his sight. **ROMANS 2:13**

It is not hard to obey when we love the one whom we obey.
ST. IGNATIUS

A child who is allowed to be disrespectful to his parents will not have true respect for anyone.
BILLY GRAHAM

True obedience is true freedom.
HENRY WARD BEECHER

Tomorrow, For Sure

Take a lesson from the ants, you lazybones. Learn from their ways and become wise!

PROVERBS 6:6

"SURE, YOU CAN GO to the amusement park with your friends on Saturday . . . *if* you get the weeding done in the flower garden before then," Mom said.

"Sure, Mom. No problem," Lacey said. It was Monday. She had five days to get the weeding done, so there was nothing to worry about.

That afternoon Lacey went to the pool with her friends. When she got home she was tired, so she vegged out in front of the TV. Tuesday was more of the same. Wednesday her mom reminded her about the weeding, and Lacey said, "I *know*, Mom." But she played video games all morning. She could have weeded in the afternoon, but she got interested in a book and then fell asleep.

Thursday it stormed all day, so it wasn't a good day for weeding.

Guess I'll do it tomorrow, Lacey thought.

But on Friday Amanda invited her to go to a movie with the other girls who were going to the amusement park. Lacey asked her mom, who just raised her eyebrow in that do-you-know-what-you're-doing way she had. "Sure, you can go," Mom said.

After the movie, the girls decided to

have a sleepover so they could get an early start the next morning. Lacey asked her mom if she could sleep over. "Sorry, but there's no amusement park for you. You didn't do the weeding."

"Moooommmm," Lacey started to complain.

"You had five days, but you kept putting it off to do things that were more fun—and now you're out of time," Mom said.

Ouch! Putting off the things you are supposed to do brings consequences. Being lazy has a price. Focusing on fun instead of work has a price. The lesson is to do your work first, and then you'll be free to have fun! God knew people would need to be reminded of this; that's why he mentioned it in the Bible.

CHECKUP TIME

On a scale of 1 to 5, how are you doing at avoiding laziness?

1 = never
2 = not very often
3 = sometimes
4 = most of the time
5 = always

I do my work before I even think about goofing off.

1   2   3   4   5

I take my responsibilities very seriously.

1   2   3   4   5

I care about the consequences for not doing my chores.

1   2   3   4   5

I know that God cares whether or not I'm lazy.

1   2   3   4   5

I think it is important for kids to have responsibilities.

1   2   3   4   5

KEY

MOSTLY 1s You are all about the fun—but God wants you to take your responsibilities seriously also. Pray for his help.

MOSTLY 2s You don't really expect other people to do everything for you, do you? Ask God to show you ways you can pitch in.

MOSTLY 3s You've seen some of the consequences for not doing your work, but maybe they haven't completely sunk in yet. Ask a parent or teacher to help you learn to be more responsible—they'll be thrilled!

MOSTLY 4s You usually do your chores on time. Keep practicing responsibility!

MOSTLY 5s Congratulations! You have learned the importance of doing your work first and having fun second!

THINGS TO DO

○ Make a chart showing which chores are your responsibility. Check off each job when you finish it.

○ If you have a big job or project, plan ahead and do a little each day so you won't be pressured by a deadline.

○ Ask your mom or dad to hold you accountable to getting your work done before fun time.

○ Thank God for the opportunity and the ability to work.

THINGS TO REMEMBER

A hard worker has plenty of food, but a person who chases fantasies has no sense. PROVERBS 12:11

Work brings profit, but mere talk leads to poverty! PROVERBS 14:23

Work willingly at whatever you do, as though you were working for the Lord rather than for people. COLOSSIANS 3:23

We hear that some of you are living idle lives, refusing to work and meddling in other people's business. We command such people and urge them in the name of the Lord Jesus Christ to settle down and work to earn their own living. 2 THESSALONIANS 3:11-12

A wise youth harvests in the summer, but one who sleeps during harvest is a disgrace. PROVERBS 10:5

Nothing will work unless you do.
MAYA ANGELOU

There is no substitute for hard work.
THOMAS EDISON

Laziness may appear attractive, but work gives satisfaction.
ANNE FRANK

How Can I Be Sure?

This is how God loved the world: He gave his one and only Son, so that everyone who believes in him will not perish but have eternal life.

JOHN 3:16

ELLIE HAS GONE TO CHURCH her whole life. Her mom teaches children's Sunday school; her dad is on the church board. Ellie likes to go because she has a lot of friends there. Her family says grace before every meal, and Dad reads Bible stories during family devotions once or twice a week; so Ellie knows a lot about God, and she knows a lot of Bible stories. When she was small her mom or dad prayed with her every night before bed. Now they just remind her to pray. Her parents love God and believe that he loves them.

But Ellie doesn't think about God much. He seems more like something for grown-ups. She knows that Jesus died for her sins, but even the whole idea of sin is kind of strange to her. She isn't sure what she does that actually qualifies as sin.

Ellie hasn't yet understood the reality of God's Good News. She doesn't get that all people—herself included—are sinners. Sin is anything we do—things like disobedience, anger, unkindness, selfishness, or theft—that breaks any of God's laws explained in the Bible. No sin is allowed in heaven because God is completely sinless. He can't have a relationship with a sinful person. Left to ourselves, no one could ever go to heaven. Everyone would go to hell when they die. But God loves people so much that he sent his Son, Jesus, who never sinned at all, to die as payment for everyone's sin. When people accept Jesus as their Savior, they accept that payment and their sins are erased! Then they can be adopted as a child of God, and he will help them and strengthen them, and someday they will go to heaven. That's what John 3:16 is all about! Have you accepted Jesus as your Savior?

CHECKUP TIME

On a scale of 1 to 5, how much do you believe in Jesus' sacrifice?

1 = never
2 = not very often
3 = sometimes
4 = most of the time
5 = always

I totally believe in Jesus and thank God for making a way for me to know him.

   1   2   3   4   5

I understand that I'm a sinner, so I'm grateful for all Jesus did.

   1   2   3   4   5

I want to know God better and better.

   1   2   3   4   5

I tell others about Jesus' sacrifice.

   1   2   3   4   5

I am grateful for having Jesus in my life.

   1   2   3   4   5

KEY

MOSTLY 1s You don't seem to understand the sacrifice and gift of Jesus at all. Ask your parents or pastor to talk with you about this.

MOSTLY 2s Do you feel like you'll have plenty of time for all this God stuff when you're older? Jesus wants to have a relationship with you now!

MOSTLY 3s Maybe you get that God loves the world. But do you get that he loves *you*? Ask him to help you understand how he feels about you.

MOSTLY 4s The Good News is making sense to you! Ask God to show you how you can follow him in your daily life.

MOSTLY 5s Praise the Lord! You have accepted Jesus as Savior and are growing in your faith and love for him!

THINGS TO DO

○ Can you remember who first told you about God's love? Thank that person—face-to-face, by phone, or in a letter.

○ Thank God for the gift of Jesus.

○ Tell someone about Jesus—even just a little bit.

○ Memorize John 3:16.

THINGS TO REMEMBER

If you openly declare that Jesus is Lord and believe in your heart that God raised him from the dead, you will be saved. For it is by believing in your heart that you are made right with God, and it is by openly declaring your faith that you are saved. **ROMANS 10:9-10**

God saved you by his grace when you believed. And you can't take credit for this; it is a gift from God. Salvation is not a reward for the good things we have done, so none of us can boast about it. **EPHESIANS 2:8-9**

Anyone who believes in God's Son has eternal life. Anyone who doesn't obey the Son will never experience eternal life but remains under God's angry judgment. **JOHN 3:36**

Jesus told him, "I am the way, the truth, and the life. No one can come to the Father except through me." **JOHN 14:6**

Look! I stand at the door and knock. If you hear my voice and open the door, I will come in, and we will share a meal together as friends. **REVELATION 3:20**

You're born. You suffer. You die. Fortunately, there's a loophole.
BILLY GRAHAM

He who created us without our help will not save us without our consent.
ST. AUGUSTINE

Jesus came to pay a debt He didn't owe because we owed a debt we couldn't pay.
UNKNOWN

Never Give Up

Take a new grip with your tired hands and strengthen your weak knees.

HEBREWS 12:12

LEANNE HAS TRIED TO BE POSITIVE and hopeful for a long time, and nothing has changed. So now . . . she is tired. It's hard to keep being hopeful when someone you love very much is sick. Leanne prays as hard as she can. She tries with all her heart to believe that God will heal Aunt Janel, but her aunt just keeps getting worse. Leanne has almost given up hope that God is even hearing her prayers. She has started asking him for one little sign that he is paying attention. Something as simple as Aunt Janel's temperature going down or her teasing Leanne like she used to. But none of that is happening—so what can Leanne do? She sort of wants to give up, but she won't, because she still believes God can heal Aunt Janel, and maybe, just maybe, if she keeps praying, he will.

It's tough to keep your hope and faith strong when someone you love is really sick. You want God to heal your loved one. You know that he can, so you keep praying and praying. But when things don't get better it's hard to stay hopeful. What do you do? Take a deep breath and remember how very much God loves you and the one you're praying for. Trust him to be with you both—no matter what happens.

If your loved one doesn't get better, God will walk through the hard times with you. If your loved one does get better, then you can praise God together. In the meantime, grab on tighter to him and hold firm!

CHECKUP TIME

On a scale of 1 to 5, how strong is your faith?

1 = never
2 = not very often
3 = sometimes
4 = most of the time
5 = always

I believe with all my heart that God hears my prayers.

1   2   3   4   5

I have seen answers to prayers.

1   2   3   4   5

I hold on tight to God, even when I'm discouraged.

1   2   3   4   5

I wait patiently for God's answers.

1   2   3   4   5

I love God whether he does what I ask or not.

1   2   3   4   5

KEY

MOSTLY 1s It sounds like your faith depends on God doing what you want him to do. Pray that he will strengthen your faith so that you can hold on to him even when things don't go the way you hope.

MOSTLY 2s Do you tend to walk away from God when you get discouraged? The next time you feel tempted to do this, pray and read the Bible even more than you normally would.

MOSTLY 3s Your faith is still on a bit of a roller coaster. Ask God to root it firmly in him.

MOSTLY 4s Pretty good. You understand there are ups and downs in life. Keep choosing to trust God!

MOSTLY 5s Good for you. You have learned to "take a new grip with your tired hands" to keep your faith strong.

THINGS TO DO

○ List some times when you absolutely knew that God answered your prayers.

○ Ask a friend to pray with you about the thing that has you concerned.

○ Research verses that promise you God is listening to your prayers.

○ Don't stop praying. Keep trusting God.

THINGS TO REMEMBER

"You don't have enough faith," Jesus told them. "I tell you the truth, if you had faith even as small as a mustard seed, you could say to this mountain, 'Move from here to there,' and it would move. Nothing would be impossible." MATTHEW 17:20

Faith shows the reality of what we hope for; it is the evidence of things we cannot see. HEBREWS 11:1

The LORD is my rock, my fortress, and my savior; my God is my rock, in whom I find protection. He is my shield, the power that saves me, and my place of safety. PSALM 18:2

The LORD is good, a strong refuge when trouble comes. He is close to those who trust in him. NAHUM 1:7

Trust in the LORD with all your heart; do not depend on your own understanding. PROVERBS 3:5

Faith isn't the ability to believe long and far into the misty future. It's simply taking God at His Word and taking the next step.
JONI EARECKSON TADA

You say to God, "I have never seen you provide for me." God says to you, "You have never trusted Me."
CORALLIE BUCHANAN

Faith all grown up is trust.
ADAM LIVECCHI

It's All a Gift

What do you have that God hasn't given you? And if everything you have is from God, why boast as though it were not a gift?

1 CORINTHIANS 4:7

LEAH IS BEAUTIFUL. There's no doubt about that. Gorgeous hair, beautiful eyes, perfect smile. She does a little modeling for a local store and buys the latest style outfits with the money she earns. She always looks like she just stepped off a fashion-show runway. Yep, she's a pretty girl. But no one wants to tell her that, because she is so proud of herself that she is annoying.

Whenever one of her friends gets a new outfit or a new haircut, Leah can't even bring herself to compliment them. She brushes off their new things with comments like, "Oh yeah, I had an outfit like that . . . last year. The newest styles are so cute, though." Or she will say, "I'd never cut my hair that short. My hair is so thick and full that it looks gorgeous when it's long and flowing." Or, "I'd never wear glasses, because they'd cover up my eyes and, well, they are just too pretty to be hidden." Ugh.

Leah acts like her beauty is something she created. But she didn't have anything to do with how beautiful she is—God gave her that. So pointing out how gorgeous her hair is or how pretty her eyes are or anything else, well, that's just bragging, and that's not good. She's putting other people down as she tries to lift herself up.

God is not a fan of bragging. And no one really has anything to brag about anyway, because in the end everything we have and everything we are is given to us by God. All people start at the same even place, which is receiving whatever God gives. So there's no reason to brag about anything—it's all a gift.

CHECKUP TIME

On a scale of 1 to 5, where are you on the humility spectrum?

1 = never
2 = not very often
3 = sometimes
4 = most of the time
5 = always

I try my best to be humble.

1 2 3 4 5

I think about whether I'm bragging before I say a word.

1 2 3 4 5

I believe God gave each person special talents and abilities.

1 2 3 4 5

I praise God for everything I am and all I have.

1 2 3 4 5

I try not to make others feel bad because of my attitudes or words.

1 2 3 4 5

KEY

MOSTLY 1s News flash—life is not all about you. Ask God to help you grow in humility.

MOSTLY 2s Humility is *not* your strong point. Remember that everything you have comes from God.

MOSTLY 3s Perhaps you know God gave you everything, but sometimes you like to brag a bit anyway? Pray that God will help you break the habit for good.

MOSTLY 4s You're generally humble, but pride sneaks in once in a while. When you feel tempted to brag, thank God instead.

MOSTLY 5s Good for you. You're giving God the credit for all you are and all you have.

THINGS TO DO

- ⭘ Make a list of all the things for which you are proud of yourself. How many of them can you honestly take credit for?

- ⭘ Make it a point to compliment another person at least twice a day.

- ⭘ Encourage a friend by pointing out the talents she has or something positive about her appearance or character that you notice.

- ⭘ Ask God to keep you humble by reminding you that everything you have is from him.

THINGS TO REMEMBER

Pride leads to disgrace,
but with humility comes wisdom.
PROVERBS 11:2

If you think you are too important to help someone, you are only fooling yourself. You are not that important. **GALATIANS 6:3**

He gives grace generously. As the Scriptures say, "God opposes the proud but gives grace to the humble." **JAMES 4:6**

Don't be selfish; don't try to impress others. Be humble, thinking of others as better than yourselves. **PHILIPPIANS 2:3**

Live in harmony with each other. Don't be too proud to enjoy the company of ordinary people. And don't think you know it all!
ROMANS 12:16

A proud man is always looking down on things and people: and, of course, as long as you are looking down, you cannot see something that is above you.
C. S. LEWIS

It is better to lose your pride with someone you love rather than to lose that someone you love with your useless pride.
JOHN RUSKIN

It was pride that changed angels into devils; it is humility that makes men as angels.
ST. AUGUSTINE

Loved beyond Belief

How precious are your thoughts about me, O God. They cannot be numbered!

I can't even count them; they outnumber the grains of sand!

And when I wake up, you are still with me!

PSALM 139:17-18

IT MADE SARA LAUGH to think about something her grandmother used to do. She and her friends would take a fresh flower and pull off the petals one at a time, saying, "He loves me" with the first petal and "He loves me not" with the second. They would pull off all the petals, and if they ended with "He loves me" then they believed that their current boyfriend loved them. It was silly, and they knew it—but it was fun.

Sara doesn't have a boyfriend, but there is someone who loves her very much—she is absolutely sure of it. Who? God, of course!

Sara knows that God thinks about her all day long. He knows where she is and what she's doing, not because he's spying on her but because he cares about her. Sara feels so happy to know that the God who made everything there is thinks about her. He knows when she is having a bad day. He knows when someone is being mean to her. He knows when she is sad. He knows when she is so overjoyed that she sings out loud. He knows when she is loving her family and friends.

Sara sees evidence of God's love all

around her. She knows that the beautiful world is a gift to people because God loves them. She knows that her family, her friends, her home, her pets, her talents . . . everything is a gift to her that comes straight from God's heart. The biggest gift of all is Jesus dying for her sins—that's the best evidence yet of God's wonderful love!

CHECKUP TIME

On a scale of 1 to 5, how loved do you feel?

1 = never
2 = not very often
3 = sometimes
4 = most of the time
5 = always

I feel God's love throughout the day.

1   2   3   4   5

Even if I can't feel God's love, I know it's there.

1   2   3   4   5

It makes me feel great to know that God thinks about me.

1   2   3   4   5

It amazes me that God—who made everything there is—loves me.

1   2   3   4   5

I am grateful for all the gifts God gives, from my family to everything in the world!

1   2   3   4   5

KEY

MOSTLY 1s Oh, no! You're missing out on God's wonderful love. Ask him to help you understand how he feels about you.

MOSTLY 2s It sounds like something is keeping you from experiencing God's love. If you don't know what it is, pray that God will show you.

MOSTLY 3s Your head knows that God loves you, but your heart is lagging behind a bit. Choose one of the activities on the next page and try to do it every day this week.

MOSTLY 4s You know what it's like to enjoy God's love! Ask him to keep reminding you how much he cares.

MOSTLY 5s Praise God! You know God loves you, and you celebrate his love each day!

THINGS TO DO

- Make a list of your favorite things that remind you of God's love.

- Thank God each day for his love and one of his special gifts to you.

- Set aside one day this week as a "thankful day," where you focus on being aware of how God shows his love to you. Encourage one or more of your friends to join you.

- Sing a song of praise to God.

THINGS TO REMEMBER

I am convinced that nothing can ever separate us from God's love. Neither death nor life, neither angels nor demons, neither our fears for today nor our worries about tomorrow—not even the powers of hell can separate us from God's love. No power in the sky above or in the earth below—indeed, nothing in all creation will ever be able to separate us from the love of God that is revealed in Christ Jesus our Lord. ROMANS 8:38-39

God showed how much he loved us by sending his one and only Son into the world so that we might have eternal life through him. This is real love—not that we loved God, but that he loved us and sent his Son as a sacrifice to take away our sins. 1 JOHN 4:9-10

Give thanks to the God of heaven. His faithful love endures forever.
PSALM 136:26

This is how God loved the world: He gave his one and only Son, so that everyone who believes in him will not perish but have eternal life.
JOHN 3:16

God showed his great love for us by sending Christ to die for us while we were still sinners.
ROMANS 5:8

God loves each of us as if there were only one of us.
ST. AUGUSTINE

God is love. He didn't need us. But he wanted us. And that is the most amazing thing.
RICK WARREN

Though our feelings come and go, His love for us does not.
C. S. LEWIS

Doing What You Can

Share your food with the hungry, and give shelter to the homeless.

Give clothes to those who need them, and do not hide from relatives who need your help.

ISAIAH 58:7

TERRA AND HER FAMILY heard the tornado siren blare, and they ran for the basement. When they got the all clear, they found out that their town was fine—but the next town over was totally destroyed. Terra couldn't believe what she saw on the news. Trees were completely pulled out of the ground. There were empty spaces where houses had been. People's belongings were flung everywhere. Families were left homeless and with no possessions. Terra was particularly touched by stories of kids her own age who suddenly had nothing. *I wonder if there is anything I can do*, she thought.

Then Terra glanced up at her closet. She had a ton of clothes. She could see about five blue shirts and four red ones just with a glance. Why did she need so many of the same color? Slowly a plan began forming in Terra's mind. *All my friends have lots of clothes too. Maybe they would be willing to give away some so that the girls who lost all their stuff could have some clothes.*

Terra checked with her friends; every one of them was willing to help! The girls started gathering clothes and separating them into sizes. Terra's church helped with handing out the clothes to the people who needed them.

What a great way to live out God's command in Isaiah 58:7! Give some of what you have to those who need it. It's God's way—people taking care of one another. We're all in this life together, so we need to pay attention to each other and help one another in any way we can.

Have you ever wondered how you can help others? Ask God to show you places where you can share.

CHECKUP TIME

On a scale of 1 to 5, how good are you at noticing needs?

1 = never
2 = not very often
3 = sometimes
4 = most of the time
5 = always

When I hear stories of people losing their homes or going through other hard situations, it touches my heart.

1   2   3   4   5

I would be completely willing to give away some of what I have to help someone else.

1   2   3   4   5

My heart aches for people who have so much less than I do.

1   2   3   4   5

I would be willing to organize an effort with my friends to help others.

1   2   3   4   5

I believe all people should help one another.

1   2   3   4   5

KEY

MOSTLY 1s Do you find yourself thinking, *That's not my problem*? God doesn't agree! Ask him to change your heart.

MOSTLY 2s Maybe your heart is so full of your own wants and problems that there's no room left for compassion. Pray that God will help you make space for loving others.

MOSTLY 3s You do see that there are people struggling in the world. That's good. Now take the next step—do what you can to help!

MOSTLY 4s You try to be compassionate and caring. Keep up the good work!

MOSTLY 5s Good for you. You have a compassionate and generous heart!

THINGS TO DO

○ Watch the news and notice how many people around the world are losing everything due to storms or wars. Ask a parent or another adult to help you find out how many people in your very own community are facing hunger or other needs.

○ Look at your own possessions. Do you have things you could share or donate to others?

○ Choose a cause and see if you can get your friends or your church to agree to help meet that need.

○ Ask God to open your eyes to those in need and show you ways you can help.

THINGS TO REMEMBER

All must give as they are able, according to the blessings given to them by the LORD your God. **DEUTERONOMY 16:17**

Blessed are those who are generous, because they feed the poor. **PROVERBS 22:9**

When you give to someone in need, don't let your left hand know what your right hand is doing. Give your gifts in private, and your Father, who sees everything, will reward you. **MATTHEW 6:3-4**

John replied, "If you have two shirts, give one to the poor. If you have food, share it with those who are hungry." **LUKE 3:11**

Suppose you see a brother or sister who has no food or clothing, and you say, "Good-bye and have a good day; stay warm and eat well"— but then you don't give that person any food or clothing. What good does that do? **JAMES 2:15-16**

You have not lived today until you have done something for someone who can never repay you.
JOHN BUNYAN

Giving frees us from the familiar territory of our own needs by opening our mind to the unexplained worlds occupied by the needs of others.
BARBARA BUSH

You will discover that you have two hands, one for helping yourself, the other for helping others.
AUDREY HEPBURN

Enough Already!

Beware! Guard against every kind of greed. Life is not measured by how much you own.

LUKE 12:15

ABBY IS DOING OKAY. She gets a pretty good allowance every week for doing chores that her parents give her. She gets paid to help out Mrs. Smith next door, who is recovering from surgery, by doing a little cleaning, watering her plants, and walking her dog. Sometimes Mrs. Dean down the street pays Abby to come play with her young children while Mrs. Dean gets some work done. Abby has more than enough money. She has a savings account, but she also keeps plenty of money in her wallet that she can spend. Yep, she is doing okay.

But there is a problem. The more money Abby gets, the more she wants. She never feels like she has enough. She holds on to every dollar. There are things she wants that she could buy herself, but she tries to talk her parents into buying them so she can save her money.

Worse than that, Abby refuses to give any of her money to help others. When her Sunday school class is collecting money to help victims of disasters, Abby doesn't give. When the offering plate is passed in church, Abby doesn't give. When it's time to buy a birthday gift for her best friend, Abby won't spend her money. You get the picture . . . Abby wants to collect

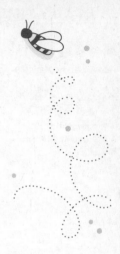

as much money as she can—and keep it. Abby is greedy—she wants everything for herself and refuses to share what she has to help or bless anyone else. That's not at all the way God wants his children to be. Grabbing more and more of something for yourself when others could use some— well, that's just selfish.

Are you generous with others, or are you always trying to keep everything for yourself?

CHECKUP TIME

On a scale of 1 to 5, how generous are you?

1 = never
2 = not very often
3 = sometimes
4 = most of the time
5 = always

I give tithes and offerings to God's work from any money I get.

1   2   3   4   5

If I have two of something, I gladly share with someone else.

1   2   3   4   5

It bothers me to see others needing things that I have a lot of.

1   2   3   4   5

I believe God means it when he says we should help one another.

1   2   3   4   5

I feel that I have enough and don't need any more clothes, money, food, or whatever.

1   2   3   4   5

KEY

MOSTLY 1s Yikes! Your greedy heart could use a major makeover. Pray that God will give you a generous heart instead.

MOSTLY 2s Think about why you are always wanting more. Ask God to help you be content with what he's already given you.

MOSTLY 3s You want to be generous, but sometimes you still struggle. Make an effort to practice generosity this week.

MOSTLY 4s You're trying to be more like your generous heavenly Father. Keep choosing to give!

MOSTLY 5s Praise God for your generous heart! You know the joy of giving!

THINGS TO DO

- ◯ Be honest with yourself. Are you ever satisfied, or do you always want more? Every day this week, thank God for the things he's given you.

- ◯ Ask God to show you ways you can be generous. Write down your ideas and put at least one of them into action this week.

- ◯ Pay attention to programs in your community where you can donate time, money, or stuff to help others.

- ◯ Take the first step—give one thing away. Then, see how you feel. You may want to give away even more!

THINGS TO REMEMBER

The love of money is the root of all kinds of evil. And some people, craving money, have wandered from the true faith and pierced themselves with many sorrows. **1 TIMOTHY 6:10**

Greed causes fighting; trusting the LORD leads to prosperity. **PROVERBS 28:25**

Don't love money; be satisfied with what you have. For God has said,

"I will never fail you. I will never abandon you." **HEBREWS 13:5**

If you give even a cup of cold water to one of the least of my followers, you will surely be rewarded. **MATTHEW 10:42**

You must each decide in your heart how much to give. And don't give reluctantly or in response to pressure. "For God loves a person who gives cheerfully." **2 CORINTHIANS 9:7**

Successful people are always looking for opportunities to help others. Unsuccessful people are always asking, "What's in it for me?"
BRIAN TRACY

He who is not contented with what he has, would not be contented with what he would like to have.
SOCRATES

Greed is a fat demon with a small mouth and whatever you feed it is never enough.
JANWILLEM VAN DE WETERING

Stormy Weather

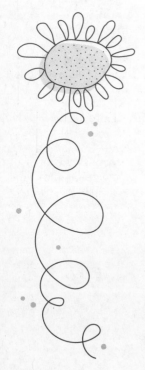

The LORD is a shelter for the oppressed, a refuge in times of trouble.
PSALM 9:9

CHRISTY UNLOCKED THE DOOR and went inside, glad to be out of the rain. She called her mom to tell her she was home, got a snack, and settled down to watch a little TV before doing her homework. A few minutes later, there was a loud crash of thunder and a flash of lightning, and just like that, the electricity went out. Christy sat in the dark listening to the driving rain, claps of thunder, and howling wind.

She hated to admit it, but fear was creeping into her heart. She fought the urge to panic, though she would have admitted to anyone who asked that she wished her mom were home. Just then she heard a siren wail, warning of the possibility of a tornado. She grabbed a flashlight and a blanket and pillow and headed for the little bathroom in the center of the house.

Huddling under the counter, Christy lost the battle to keep her panic under control. Her heart raced and her stomach was in knots. She didn't think she had ever been more afraid or felt more alone.

Christy is in a scary situation, there's no doubt about that. And it's understandable that she feels alone. But . . . she's not. Sometimes when we're really scared and longing to have a parent or another adult with us for protection, we forget that God is there. He's always with us. Nothing will happen to us that God doesn't know about.

It's important to remember that God is protecting, guarding, and loving you no matter what situation you're facing. It's okay if you feel scared, but remind yourself that you're not alone. God is there. God knows.

CHECKUP TIME

On a scale of 1 to 5, how aware are you of God's presence?

1 = never
2 = not very often
3 = sometimes
4 = most of the time
5 = always

When I am scared, I remember right away that God is with me.

1 2 3 4 5

It comforts me to read Bible verses and sing praise choruses when I'm frightened.

1 2 3 4 5

I pray for an awareness of God's presence to comfort me.

1 2 3 4 5

I believe God is watching out for me.

1 2 3 4 5

I'm finding that the more I trust God, the less afraid I feel.

1 2 3 4 5

KEY

MOSTLY 1s Living in fear is no way to live! Pray right now that God will help you learn to trust him.

MOSTLY 2s Fear doesn't have to control you! Remember that God is much bigger than your fears.

MOSTLY 3s You know that you can trust God, but sometimes it's hard to do. Pick at least one of the actions on the next page and do it this week.

MOSTLY 4s You usually trust God with your fears. Keep choosing to put your faith in him.

MOSTLY 5s You trust God to always be with you. Doesn't it feel great to be free from fear?

THINGS TO DO

○ Think about what kinds of situations make you afraid. Do you really think that there's anything you're facing that God can't help you with?

○ List some verses that talk about how God promises to be with you.

○ Pray and ask God to take away your fear, and remember that he is in control.

○ Memorize a verse that you can repeat when you start feeling afraid.

THINGS TO REMEMBER

O my people, trust in him at all times. Pour out your heart to him, for God is our refuge. **PSALM 62:8**

God has not given us a spirit of fear and timidity, but of power, love, and self-discipline. **2 TIMOTHY 1:7**

I prayed to the LORD, and he answered me. He freed me from all my fears. **PSALM 34:4**

When I am afraid,
I will put my trust in you.
I praise God for what he has promised.
I trust in God, so why should I be afraid?
What can mere mortals do to me?
PSALM 56:3-4

Such love has no fear, because perfect love expels all fear. If we are afraid, it is for fear of punishment, and this shows that we have not fully experienced his perfect love. **1 JOHN 4:18**

Fear is the highest fence.
DUDLEY NICHOLS

Worry is interest paid on trouble before it comes due.
WILLIAM RALPH INGE

The greatest sense of love, which is available for us at all times, is God's love.
STORMIE OMARTIAN

Bad Company

> Putting confidence in an unreliable person in times of trouble is like chewing with a broken tooth or walking on a lame foot.
>
> PROVERBS 25:19

"KELSIE INVITED ME to a sleepover on Friday night. Can I go, can I? Please? I can't believe she asked me. I've wanted to be in her group for, like, forever!" Cori begged.

"Will her parents be home?" Mom asked. Typical Mom question.

"Yep. She said they would be there. She said we would watch movies and do our nails. It's going to be so fun!" Cori said.

Cori really wanted to be accepted into Kelsie's group of friends. They were the top group at school. All the girls wanted to be like them and hang out with them.

Cori went to the sleepover, but things did not turn out the way she expected. A couple of Kelsie's other friends were there, and as soon as they were in Kelsie's room with the door closed, they got on Kelsie's computer and started posting mean comments online about people they knew. Cori tried to be cool at first. Then she pulled out her nail polish and tried to suggest a movie or anything else to do, but Kelsie and her friends made fun of her for being a baby.

Why did I want to be friends with these girls? Cori wondered. *Why did I think they were so cool?*

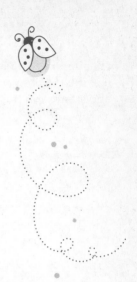

It's easy to get your priorities messed up, isn't it? Being in Kelsie's group was so important to Cori that she didn't see any warning signs that they probably didn't share her values. If obeying and serving God are important to you, then you want to stay out of situations where you may be tempted to do things you know wouldn't please him. Be careful. Keep your eyes on God and don't get blinded by anything or anyone else, no matter how cool they seem to be!

CHECKUP TIME

On a scale of 1 to 5, how careful are you about who you trust?

1 = never
2 = not very often
3 = sometimes
4 = most of the time
5 = always

I make sure that people I trust have a strong faith in God.

1   2   3   4   5

I listen to my parents' advice more than to anyone else.

1   2   3   4   5

When I get advice, I match it against God's Word to see if it agrees.

1   2   3   4   5

If I have to choose between my friends or God, I choose God.

1   2   3   4   5

I'm careful to choose friends who have the same values I have.

1   2   3   4   5

KEY

MOSTLY 1s You're walking around with a blindfold on, and sooner or later you're going to get hurt. Ask God to help you choose trustworthy friends.

MOSTLY 2s You need some help with this. Talk with a parent or another adult you are close to about why who you trust matters.

MOSTLY 3s You try to make good choices about who you put your trust in, but your judgment isn't always the best. Pray that God will give you wisdom.

MOSTLY 4s You know that having trustworthy friends is important. Ask God to help you resist the temptation you might still feel to run after what's cool instead of what's right.

MOSTLY 5s Nice! You are careful to make sure that the people you trust share your values and your faith in God.

THINGS TO DO

○ Think about the people you take advice from. Who gives good advice and who doesn't? Decide to start spending your time with those who give good advice.

○ Make a list of people you know who love God and who you can trust to give you honest answers and wise advice.

○ Research Bible verses on wisdom. Memorize at least one of them this week.

○ Ask God to give you wisdom in what advice you take to heart.

THINGS TO REMEMBER

If you listen to constructive criticism, you will be at home among the wise.
PROVERBS 15:31

Get all the advice and instruction you can, so you will be wise the rest of your life.
PROVERBS 19:20

Fear of the LORD is the foundation of wisdom. Knowledge of the Holy One results in good judgment. **PROVERBS 9:10**

Jesus Christ is the same yesterday, today, and forever. **HEBREWS 13:8**

Oh, the joys of those who do not
follow the advice of the wicked,
or stand around with sinners,
or join in with mockers.
But they delight in the law of the LORD,
meditating on it day and night.
PSALM 1:1-2

Advice is like mushrooms. The wrong kind can prove fatal.
E. C. MCKENZIE

If you listen too much to advice, you may wind up making other people's mistakes.
CROFT M. PENTZ

Nobody can go back and start a new beginning, but anyone can start today and make a new ending.
MARIA ROBINSON

When, God, When?

As soon as I pray,
you answer me;
you encourage me by
giving me strength.

PSALM 138:3

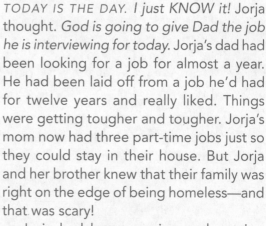

TODAY IS THE DAY. I just KNOW it! Jorja thought. *God is going to give Dad the job he is interviewing for today.* Jorja's dad had been looking for a job for almost a year. He had been laid off from a job he'd had for twelve years and really liked. Things were getting tougher and tougher. Jorja's mom now had three part-time jobs just so they could stay in their house. But Jorja and her brother knew that their family was right on the edge of being homeless—and that was scary!

Jorja had been praying and praying for her dad. She believed God answers prayers. She was the only one in her family who was a Christian, and she thought that if God would somehow come through with a great job for her dad, then maybe her family would start believing in God too.

The interview came and went. The days passed. The weeks passed. There was no job offer for Jorja's dad. Jorja felt disappointed. Sad. Angry. Confused. Alone. It seemed like a bazillion emotions were flying around in her heart and mind. Jorja believed that God answers prayer . . . but she was confused as to why her prayer wasn't answered.

It is confusing when your prayers seem

to be accomplishing nothing, isn't it? Do you have trouble remembering that God is listening and that he cares? Of course you wish he would act more quickly, but God works within his own time frame, and you can't change that. You just have to remember that he is listening and he does care. And he will answer your prayer in his way and in his time. Waiting is hard, but keep reminding yourself of his love and care. Hang on tight to that!

CHECKUP TIME

On a scale of 1 to 5, how confident are you that God answers prayer?

1 = never
2 = not very often
3 = sometimes
4 = most of the time
5 = always

I believe that God hears every one of my prayers.

1   2   3   4   5

I pray about everything that comes to mind.

1   2   3   4   5

I trust God even when he doesn't answer prayers the way I want.

1   2   3   4   5

I keep praying for things, even when I don't see God's answers.

1   2   3   4   5

I believe God does what is best for me and those I love.

1   2   3   4   5

KEY

MOSTLY 1s Whoa. You are having some trouble believing that God answers prayer! Ask him to help you understand how much he cares about you.

MOSTLY 2s Sounds like it's hard for you to believe in the power of prayer. Ask a friend or a parent to tell you about a time when God answered their prayers.

MOSTLY 3s It's easy to trust God when he answers the way you want him to, but you need to trust him even when you don't get the answer you want. Pray that he will help you do that.

MOSTLY 4s You're doing pretty well putting your faith in God all the time. Keep on praying and trusting!

MOSTLY 5s Good for you! You trust God to hear your prayers, and you trust his answers.

THINGS TO DO

○ Make a prayer journal. Write down your requests and date them. Mark when God answers your prayers.

○ Write out verses on prayer that show God's promise to hear and answer. Try to memorize at least one.

○ Talk with a trusted adult about prayer. Ask that person about a time when God didn't answer a prayer the way he or she wanted him to and how that person knew that God still loved him or her.

○ Write a list of ways you have seen God answer prayers in the past.

THINGS TO REMEMBER

Keep on asking, and you will receive what you ask for. Keep on seeking, and you will find. Keep on knocking, and the door will be opened to you. MATTHEW 7:7

Pray in the Spirit at all times and on every occasion. Stay alert and be persistent in your prayers for all believers everywhere. EPHESIANS 6:18

[The Lord said,] "If my people who are called by my name will humble themselves and pray and seek my face and turn from their wicked ways, I will hear from heaven and will forgive their sins and restore their land." 2 CHRONICLES 7:14

We are confident that [the Son of God] hears us whenever we ask for anything that pleases him. And since we know he hears us when we make our requests, we also know that he will give us what we ask for. 1 JOHN 5:14-15

Never stop praying. 1 THESSALONIANS 5:17

The fewer words, the better the prayer.
MARTIN LUTHER

Don't pray when you feel like it. Have an appointment with the Lord and keep it. A man is powerful on his knees.
CORRIE TEN BOOM

Prayer is where the action is.
JOHN WESLEY

Gram's Hands

We have not stopped praying for you since we first heard about you. We ask God to give you complete knowledge of his will and to give you spiritual wisdom and understanding.

COLOSSIANS 1:9

ELLA LOVES HANGING OUT with her grandmother, or Gram, as she calls her. They enjoy doing many of the same things—going to the theater, eating frozen yogurt, and shopping. They have a lot of fun together. Gram loves to teach Ella how to do things like bake homemade bread. Gram shows Ella how to mix the ingredients and how to knead the dough. It's really cool. Ella can't wait to taste some of their yummy, fresh bread!

While Ella is watching Gram, she notices something kind of interesting— Gram's hands. There are light brown spots on her hands. She calls them age spots and says there is one for every time one of her kids had a problem. Her knuckles are kind of big because of arthritis, and Ella knows they hurt sometimes. Gram keeps her fingernails short because that's easier for working in the garden. Gram is always busy, and her hands show that she uses them to do a lot of different things.

Gram's hands are sometimes gentle and loving, like when she rocks Ella's baby cousin. They can be strong, like when she weeds her garden. They can be enthusiastic, like when she applauds after a play at the theater. But there's one thing Gram's hands do that Ella appreciates the most—that's when Gram folds them in prayer. Ella knows that Gram prays for her every day, sometimes many times a day, and she is so thankful to have a grandmother who faithfully prays for her family. Gram reads her Bible every day and teaches Ella about living for God by the way she acts and the words she speaks. Ella believes that Gram's prayers have helped her own faith in God grow stronger.

CHECKUP TIME

On a scale of 1 to 5, how do you feel about someone praying for you?

1 = never
2 = not very often
3 = sometimes
4 = most of the time
5 = always

I know that there is at least one person who prays for me regularly.

1   2   3   4   5

It makes me feel good to know that someone is praying for me.

1   2   3   4   5

I pray for other people on a daily basis.

1   2   3   4   5

I believe that my life is changed because of people praying for me.

1   2   3   4   5

I believe that prayer makes a difference.

1   2   3   4   5

KEY

MOSTLY 1s You need some reminders about the power of prayer! Ask a relative, teacher, or friend about how prayer has changed his or her life.

MOSTLY 2s Maybe you feel like prayer works for other people but doesn't apply to you. Ask God to help you see how prayer makes a difference in your life.

MOSTLY 3s You know that prayer is important, but sometimes other things get in the way. Memorize a Bible verse about prayer.

MOSTLY 4s You're getting it—prayer makes a difference. Make it a habit to pray every day!

MOSTLY 5s Great! You thank God for all those who pray for you and remember to pray for others, too!

THINGS TO DO

- ○ Stop and think about who prays for you. A grandparent? A parent? A friend? Thank God for that person.

- ○ Write a thank-you note to someone you know who prays for you.

- ○ Choose someone you can pray for each day.

- ○ Ask God to remind you of the power of prayer.

THINGS TO REMEMBER

Confess your sins to each other and pray for each other so that you may be healed. The earnest prayer of a righteous person has great power and produces wonderful results. **JAMES 5:16**

I urge you, first of all, to pray for all people. Ask God to help them; intercede on their behalf, and give thanks for them. **1 TIMOTHY 2:1**

Devote yourselves to prayer with an alert mind and a thankful heart. **COLOSSIANS 4:2**

If you remain in me and my words remain in you, you may ask for anything you want, and it will be granted! **JOHN 15:7**

Dear brothers and sisters, we ask you to pray for us. Pray that the Lord's message will spread rapidly and be honored wherever it goes, just as when it came to you. **2 THESSALONIANS 3:1**

Prayer is not asking. Prayer is putting oneself in the hands of God, at His disposition, and listening to His voice in the depth of our hearts.
MOTHER TERESA

In prayer it is better to have a heart without words than words without a heart.
JOHN BUNYAN

He that loveth little prayeth little, he that loveth much prayeth much.
ST. AUGUSTINE

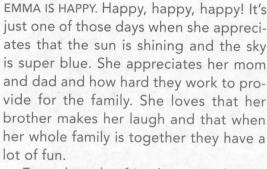

Happy, Happy, Happy!

I will praise God's name with singing, and I will honor him with thanksgiving.

PSALM 69:30

EMMA IS HAPPY. Happy, happy, happy! It's just one of those days when she appreciates that the sun is shining and the sky is super blue. She appreciates her mom and dad and how hard they work to provide for the family. She loves that her brother makes her laugh and that when her whole family is together they have a lot of fun.

Emma loves her friends, too. Today she is thankful for every one of them. Some friends are really great listeners. Some like to play softball with Emma. Some like the same kind of music. Some are Christians, and Emma likes talking about God and praying with these friends.

Emma is thankful for her favorite things in God's creation, like the tall oak tree in her backyard. It's fun to climb. She loves the mountains and thinks they show God's amazing strength. Emma likes the beach, where the ocean waves come lapping at the shore. The ocean is so big she can't help but be reminded of God. But Emma can't see the mountains and ocean every day, so on thankful days like this one she appreciates seeing God's creativity in the beautiful flowers in her mom's garden. She is amazed at how God thought to wrap

flower petals around one another to make a gorgeous rose.

Do you have happy days like Emma's? It's good to stop in the middle of your busy life and just appreciate all the good things God gives. Take time to enjoy those people and things. Enjoy his creation. Enjoy his blessings. And, as you're enjoying them, be sure to thank him. It's nice to let him know that you appreciate and enjoy all he gives you!

CHECKUP TIME

On a scale of 1 to 5, how often do you praise God?

1 = never
2 = not very often
3 = sometimes
4 = most of the time
5 = always

I have days when I feel full of praise!

1   2   3   4   5

When I'm feeling happy, I remember to praise God.

1   2   3   4   5

I give God credit for the things I enjoy.

1   2   3   4   5

I thank God as well as make requests.

1   2   3   4   5

I take time to enjoy God's creation.

1   2   3   4   5

KEY

MOSTLY 1s Ouch! That grumpy attitude of yours doesn't do you or anyone else any good. Ask God to turn your heart around and help you have a thankful attitude.

MOSTLY 2s There are a few glimmers of sunshine peeking through, but your outlook is still mostly cloudy. Try to find three things to thank God for every day.

MOSTLY 3s Sometimes you remember to praise God for what he's given you, but sometimes you forget. When you feel tempted to complain, think of something you can thank him for instead.

MOSTLY 4s You're thankful and joyful most of the time. Keep practicing praise!

MOSTLY 5s Woo-hoo! Celebrate! You know that God is good, and you make it a habit to thank him for it!

THINGS TO DO

○ Thank God for your favorite part of creation.

○ Thank God for your family and friends.

○ Thank God for your pets or for your favorite possessions.

○ Thank God for his love and care.

THINGS TO REMEMBER

Sing to him; yes, sing his praises. Tell everyone about his wonderful deeds. **1 CHRONICLES 16:9**

O my Strength, to you I sing praises, for you, O God, are my refuge, the God who shows me unfailing love.
PSALM 59:17

I will praise the LORD as long as I live. I will sing praises to my God with my dying breath. **PSALM 146:2**

Great is the LORD! He is most worthy of praise! No one can measure his greatness.
PSALM 145:3

All praise to God, the Father of our Lord Jesus Christ. It is by his great mercy that we have been born again, because God raised Jesus Christ from the dead. **1 PETER 1:3**

Even if God never did another good thing in our lives, we could spend the rest of this life praising Him for what He has already done.
DILLON BURROUGHS

The most valuable thing the Psalms do for me is to express the same delight in God which made David dance.
C. S. LEWIS

Worship is an it-is-well-with-my-soul experience.
ROBERT E. WEBBER

Thankful for God's Forgiveness

If we confess our sins to him, he is faithful and just to forgive us our sins and to cleanse us from all wickedness.

1 JOHN 1:9

JANA QUIETLY CLOSED the front door and slowly climbed the stairs to her room. She stretched out on her bed and closed her eyes. *What is wrong with me?* she wondered. *I keep doing the same thing over and over. I want so much to be kind and helpful and to obey God, but I keep doing the same dumb things. Sometimes I think I should just quit. I don't know why God would want me around anyway.*

Jana's mother knocked softly on the door and came into the room. "Honey, what's the matter?" she asked. Jana started to cry, and slowly the whole story came out. She confessed to her mom how she repeatedly did the same bad things over and over.

"Mom, I have to keep asking God to forgive me again and again," Jana moaned. "What if he gets tired of it and just stops forgiving me?"

Jana's mother hugged her tight. "Jana, sweetheart, that is never going to happen. God loves you very, very much. He will keep forgiving you as often as you ask. That's because he looks at your heart and sees that you really want to obey him. Let's thank him for his forgiveness right now."

Jana's mother is very wise. She knows

that God's forgiveness has no end. He will forgive you as many times as you ask him, because he loves you. Isn't that wonderful news?

Why not stop and thank God for his forgiveness right now? Thank him that he will forgive you even when you do the same things over and over. Thank him for seeing in your heart that you truly want to be obedient to him. God knows that living for him is a journey and that the longer you know him the better you will get at it.

CHECKUP TIME

On a scale of 1 to 5, how thankful are you for God's forgiveness?

1 = never
2 = not very often
3 = sometimes
4 = most of the time
5 = always

I know I need forgiveness every day.

1   2   3   4   5

I am confident that God will never get tired of forgiving me.

1   2   3   4   5

I try really hard to stop doing things I know are wrong.

1   2   3   4   5

I'm thankful for God's forgiveness.

1   2   3   4   5

When I ask for God's forgiveness, I am really sorry for my sin.

1   2   3   4   5

KEY

MOSTLY 1s You have a lot to learn about forgiveness. Read over the verses on the next page every day this week. Ask God to teach you about his forgiveness.

MOSTLY 2s Are you carrying around guilt about something you did? Talk to a parent or another trusted adult about it.

MOSTLY 3s You know that you're forgiven, but sometimes guilt and shame still creep in. Memorize Psalm 103:12 and say it to yourself whenever that happens.

MOSTLY 4s You have experienced the joy that comes from God's forgiveness. Keep reminding yourself of his forever love!

MOSTLY 5s Praise the Lord! You get it! You are living forgiven and free!

THINGS TO DO

○ Try to remember the last time you asked for forgiveness. What was it for?

○ If there is something you need to ask God to forgive right now, ask him. Don't wait any longer!

○ Tell God thanks for his forgiveness.

○ Memorize 1 John 1:9.

THINGS TO REMEMBER

I—yes, I alone—will blot out
your sins for my own sake
and will never think of them again.
ISAIAH 43:25

"Come now, let's settle this," says the LORD.
"Though your sins are like scarlet,
I will make them as white as snow.
Though they are red like crimson,
I will make them as white as wool."
ISAIAH 1:18

He has removed our sins as far from us
as the east is from the west. **PSALM 103:12**

Where is another God like you,
who pardons the guilt of the remnant,
overlooking the sins of his special people?
You will not stay angry with your people forever,
because you delight in showing unfailing
love. **MICAH 7:18**

This is my blood, which confirms the covenant
between God and his people. It is poured out
as a sacrifice to forgive the sins of many.
MATTHEW 26:28

*After grief for sin there
should be joy for
forgiveness.*
A. W. PINK

*Our love for God and
our appreciation of His
love and forgiveness will
be in proportion to the
recognition of our sin
and unworthiness.*
DAVE HUNT

*Man has two great
spiritual needs. One
is for forgiveness. The
other is for goodness.*
BILLY GRAHAM

Who You Gonna Listen To?

*It is better to take
refuge in the LORD
than to trust in people.*

PSALM 118:8

GINNY DOESN'T KNOW WHAT TO DO. A couple of her friends are trying to talk her into doing something that she knows is wrong. They know it is wrong too, because they are keeping it a secret from their parents. Ginny doesn't want her friends to think she is a baby. She is afraid that if she doesn't go along with them they will stop being her friend.

Ginny knows she needs someone to give her good advice, so she goes to her grandmother. They have a good connection, and Ginny always feels that she gets good advice from her wise grandma.

Grandma listens as Ginny explains the whole situation—what her friends want her to do and how she feels about it. She listens as Ginny worries about her friends leaving her and how scary it would be to not have those friends.

When Ginny has told the whole story, she asks, "Grandma, what should I do?"

Grandma thinks for a moment before responding. "If these girls are asking you to do something that you know is wrong— something that could get you in trouble— do you think they are really good friends? Real friends want the best for their friends. They don't try to get them in trouble.

I know you are scared to lose these friends, but do you think they are really the best people for you to spend time with?"

That's all Grandma says, but she has given Ginny plenty to think about. She doesn't tell Ginny what to do, but she points out things that Ginny hasn't thought about.

It's important to talk to someone older and wiser when you have a big decision to make. That's the way to get good advice and help in making wise choices.

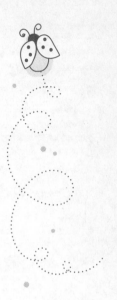

CHECKUP TIME

On a scale of 1 to 5, how thankful are you for wise friends?

1 = never
2 = not very often
3 = sometimes
4 = most of the time
5 = always

I appreciate the advice of those older and wiser than me.

1   2   3   4   5

I need all the advice I can get.

1   2   3   4   5

I take wise advice—even if it isn't what I want to hear.

1   2   3   4   5

Advice makes me think about things differently.

1   2   3   4   5

I'm thankful for the people God put in my life who can give me advice.

1   2   3   4   5

KEY

MOSTLY 1s A know-it-all attitude is going to get you in trouble sooner or later. God has put people in your life to help you. It's time to start listening to them!

MOSTLY 2s You listen to advice every now and then, but deep down you still think you know best. Ask God to help you recognize when you should listen to someone else.

MOSTLY 3s You know that it's important to listen to wise advice, but sometimes you prefer your own way. Are you facing an important decision? Get input from someone wiser than you.

MOSTLY 4s You know that you need good advice in your life. Keep running after wisdom!

MOSTLY 5s You listen to the good advisers God has put in your life! That's a sign of wisdom and maturity!

THINGS TO DO

○ Is there something going on in your life right now that you could use advice about? Ask someone you trust for input, even if you think you already know what to do.

○ Make a list of some older people you know whose advice might be helpful. Sometimes it's easy to feel like older people don't really understand you, but they've probably dealt with many of the same things you're facing. Older Christians have wisdom that comes from years of following God.

○ Ask God to direct you to the right people to talk with.

○ Thank God for people you can go to for advice.

THINGS TO REMEMBER

Fear of the LORD is the foundation of true knowledge, but fools despise wisdom and discipline. **PROVERBS 1:7**

I searched everywhere, determined to find wisdom and to understand the reason for things. I was determined to prove to myself that wickedness is stupid and that foolishness is madness. **ECCLESIASTES 7:25**

Instruct the wise,
and they will be even wiser.
Teach the righteous,
and they will learn even more. **PROVERBS 9:9**

Be careful how you live. Don't live like fools, but like those who are wise. **EPHESIANS 5:15**

Those who are wise will take all this to heart; they will see in our history the faithful love of the LORD. **PSALM 107:43**

Patience is the companion of wisdom.
ST. AUGUSTINE

The years teach much which the days never know.
RALPH WALDO EMERSON

A single conversation with a wise man is better than ten years of study.
CHINESE PROVERB

Loved Forever!

I am convinced that nothing can ever separate us from God's love. Neither death nor life, neither angels nor demons, neither our fears for today nor our worries about tomorrow—not even the powers of hell can separate us from God's love.
ROMANS 8:38

NOELLE FEELS ALONE. Not just alone, but lonely. Her best friend's family just moved all the way across the country. Noelle misses Lila so much that her heart aches. To top it off, it turns out that the other girls in their group had been friends with Noelle just because of Lila, and now that Lila is gone, so are they. So, yeah, Noelle is alone . . . and lonely.

Why don't I have friends? she wonders. *Why were those girls just friends with me because of Lila? Am I that awful?*

Now Noelle eats lunch alone. She rides the school bus alone. She goes home after school and sits . . . alone. After a few days of this, Noelle feels that no one could possibly love her—maybe not even her family.

Noelle is feeling very alone because she has forgotten that there is someone who is *always* with her—God. But while there's no doubt that God's presence is important, what Noelle really wants is a flesh-and-blood friend. So what does she do?

First, Noelle focuses on the reality that God is with her . . . always. He loves her. He never leaves her alone. He cares about her loneliness.

Second, Noelle asks God to help her

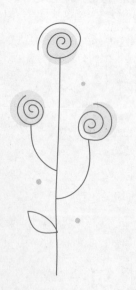

find friends who will like her for who she is—not just because she is Lila's friend.

The important thing to remember when you feel alone is that . . . you aren't. God promises to always be with you, too. He knows what you're going through. He knows if you're lonely or scared or filled with joy. And he cares.

CHECKUP TIME

On a scale of 1 to 5, do you believe God loves you always, no matter what?

1 = never
2 = not very often
3 = sometimes
4 = most of the time
5 = always

When I'm lonely or sad, I remind myself of God's love.

    1   **2**   **3**   **4**   **5**

I see evidence of God's love all around me.

    1   **2**   **3**   **4**   **5**

I tell others that God's love is constant.

    1   **2**   **3**   **4**   **5**

I believe God's love is unconditional.

    1   **2**   **3**   **4**   **5**

I know God cares when I'm sad or lonely.

    1   **2**   **3**   **4**   **5**

KEY

MOSTLY 1s You don't need to feel so alone. God does care! Talk to him. Tell him about your troubles.

MOSTLY 2s You're having a hard time remembering God's love. Memorize a Bible verse that talks about how much he loves you. Say it to yourself when you feel lonely.

MOSTLY 3s Remind yourself that God loves you in hard times as well as good times.

MOSTLY 4s You know that you can depend on God's love no matter what. Ask him to help you really live like you believe that.

MOSTLY 5s Hooray! You do understand God's love!

THINGS TO DO

○ Research Bible promises of God's love.

○ Talk with God and a trusted adult about your feelings.

○ Memorize a verse that promises God's constant love.

○ Write down evidences you see of God's love. Maybe you feel God's love in hugs from your mom or dad, or see it in wildflowers during spring.

THINGS TO REMEMBER

God showed his great love for us by sending Christ to die for us while we were still sinners. ROMANS 5:8

God showed how much he loved us by sending his one and only Son into the world so that we might have eternal life through him. This is real love—not that we loved God, but that he loved us and sent his Son as a sacrifice to take away our sins. 1 JOHN 4:9-10

The LORD your God is living among you.
He is a mighty savior.
He will take delight in you with gladness.
With his love, he will calm all your fears.
He will rejoice over you with joyful songs.
ZEPHANIAH 3:17

See how very much our Father loves us, for he calls us his children, and that is what we are! But the people who belong to this world don't recognize that we are God's children because they don't know him. 1 JOHN 3:1

Give thanks to the God of heaven.
His faithful love endures forever.
PSALM 136:26

> Trust the past to God's mercy, the present to God's love, and the future to God's providence.
> ST. AUGUSTINE

> Peace on the outside comes from knowing God on the inside.
> UNKNOWN

> Nothing can separate you from God's love, absolutely nothing. . . . God is enough for time, God is enough for eternity. God is enough!
> HANNAH WHITALL SMITH

Sick and Tired

Great is his faithfulness;
his mercies begin
afresh each morning.
LAMENTATIONS 3:23

BRIANA DIDN'T FEEL GOOD. She had not been feeling well for quite a while. When her mom took her to the doctor, he ordered a bunch of tests. It wasn't much fun to go through all of them. The tests revealed that Briana had a pretty serious problem. She was put in the hospital to receive lots of super doses of medicine and then to have more tests to see how she was doing.

Briana was tired of feeling bad, and she was scared. "What will happen if the medicine doesn't work? How long will I have to be in the hospital? Will I ever get to hang out with my friends again? Could I even die because of this?" Those kinds of thoughts raced around Briana's mind.

Who could blame Briana for being scared? Being sick is no fun, and being seriously sick for a long time can be frightening. If you've ever been sick—or been praying for someone who was sick—you know that illness can seem to go on forever. The best thing to do when you're sick is pray. One of God's names is "the Great Physician"—that means he is the smartest, most accomplished, most trustworthy doctor *ever*. He can heal anything, even things that human doctors don't know how to treat. Admit to him that you are scared. It's okay; he understands that. Ask him to remind you that he is close to you and taking care of you.

Another good thing to do is obey what your doctor tells you. God has given him or her the wisdom and training to care for you. So depend on God and listen to your doctor!

CHECKUP TIME

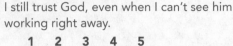

On a scale of 1 to 5, how well do you trust God when you're scared for your health or your future?

1 = never
2 = not very often
3 = sometimes
4 = most of the time
5 = always

I still trust God, even when I can't see him working right away.

1   2   3   4   5

I start each day by reminding myself of God's love.

1   2   3   4   5

The first thing I do when I'm afraid is pray.

1   2   3   4   5

I have an adult I can talk with about my fears.

1   2   3   4   5

I believe God has good plans for my future.

1   2   3   4   5

KEY

MOSTLY 1s It's normal to feel scared when times are tough, but God doesn't want you to live in fear! Cry out to him for help.

MOSTLY 2s Talk with someone you trust about your fears. Ask this person to pray with you and for you.

MOSTLY 3s You know that God can be trusted, but your heart still feels afraid sometimes. Memorize one of the verses on the next page and say it when you feel afraid.

MOSTLY 4s You're winning the battle against fear. Keep fighting back with God's power!

MOSTLY 5s Great! You trust God even in hard times.

THINGS TO DO

○ Make a list of people you can talk with when you are afraid.

○ Write down things that are scaring you—face your fears. You might discover that they're not as scary once you bring them into the open.

○ Memorize a verse like Lamentations 3:23 to hold on to when you're scared.

○ Begin every morning by thanking God for his love and protection.

THINGS TO REMEMBER

"I know the plans I have for you," says the LORD. "They are plans for good and not for disaster, to give you a future and a hope." JEREMIAH 29:11

We never give up. Though our bodies are dying, our spirits are being renewed every day. For our present troubles are small and won't last very long. Yet they produce for us a glory that vastly outweighs them and will last forever! So we don't look at the troubles we can see now; rather, we fix our gaze on things that cannot be seen. For the things we see now will soon be gone, but the things we cannot see will last forever. 2 CORINTHIANS 4:16-18

Rejoice in our confident hope. Be patient in trouble, and keep on praying. ROMANS 12:12

Faith shows the reality of what we hope for; it is the evidence of things we cannot see. HEBREWS 11:1

Trust in the LORD with all your heart; do not depend on your own understanding. PROVERBS 3:5

Where hope would otherwise become hopelessness, it becomes faith.
ROBERT BRAULT

Once you choose hope, anything's possible.
CHRISTOPHER REEVE

Hope begins in the dark, the stubborn hope that if you just show up and try to do the right thing, the dawn will come.
ANNE LAMOTT

The Best Me I Can Be

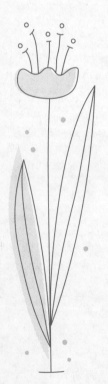

LEXI LISTENED AS KAIYA SANG. She had a beautiful voice. Everyone loved hearing Kaiya sing. Later Lexi watched Hannah playing soccer. She was so good. No one could keep up with her as she raced down the field. That night Lexi worked on her math homework. She struggled so hard to understand math. It just didn't make sense to her. *I wish I could be as good at math as Erica is. She gets it. She's at the top of our class*, Lexi thought.

Each time Lexi thinks about one of her friends and her particular skills, she feels . . . less than. She wishes she could sing like Kaiya or be athletic like Hannah or be smart like Erica. Lexi just doesn't feel that she is good at anything. She feels like she is nothing special.

See what Lexi is doing? She's comparing herself to those around her. That's never a good idea. She will always find a way to come up short in a comparison like that. Lexi would do better to look at her own interests and abilities and work on improving them.

Do you sometimes do the same kind of thing Lexi is doing? Do you wish you were more like one of your friends? Do you feel that you aren't good at anything? What does that say about how God made you? Did he make a mistake when he created you? Nope. He did not. It's better to focus on your own interests and abilities. Enjoy them. Work on them so that you get even better at them. Not sure what they are? Ask your friends and family what they think you're good at. Think about the things you love doing. Maybe you are good at being a caring friend. Maybe you enjoy cooking or sewing. Maybe you're good at planning things or remembering things. God wants you to be the best *you* that you can be.

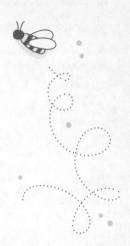

CHECKUP TIME

On a scale of 1 to 5, how do you feel about the *you* God made?

1 = never
2 = not very often
3 = sometimes
4 = most of the time
5 = always

I know I am good enough the way I am.

1   2   3   4   5

I resist the temptation to compare myself to others.

1   2   3   4   5

I know what my good qualities are and what I enjoy doing.

1   2   3   4   5

I believe God made me just the way he wants me to be.

1   2   3   4   5

I know that God does not make mistakes.

1   2   3   4   5

KEY

MOSTLY 1s God does not want you to be so down on the you he made and loves. Ask him to help you see yourself through his eyes.

MOSTLY 2s Stop comparing yourself to others! What's one good thing about *you* that you can focus on today?

MOSTLY 3s You know that God made you the way he wanted you, but sometimes you still feel tempted to put yourself down. Pray that God will help you fight back with his truth.

MOSTLY 4s You usually feel like the lovely and unique young lady God made you to be! Keep working on the strengths he gave you!

MOSTLY 5s Hooray! You love being the best you that you can be!

THINGS TO DO

○ Choose one thing you're good at and that you enjoy. Write down ways you can get even better at it or use it to help someone else.

○ Can you think of a reason that you're not happy with yourself? Talk to one of your parents or a wise friend about it.

○ Memorize Psalm 139:14. God made you just the way he wants you to be!

○ Thank God for your talents, abilities, interests, and strengths. Thank him for making *you*!

THINGS TO REMEMBER

I knew you before I formed you
in your mother's womb.
Before you were born I set you apart
and appointed you as my prophet to
the nations. Jeremiah 1:5

How precious are your thoughts about me,
O God.
They cannot be numbered! PSALM 139:17

The very hairs on your head are all numbered.
So don't be afraid; you are more valuable to
God than a whole flock of sparrows.
MATTHEW 10:30-31

God has given each of you a gift from his great
variety of spiritual gifts. Use them well to serve
one another. 1 PETER 4:10

Because of the privilege and authority God
has given me, I give each of you this warning:
Don't think you are better than you really are.
Be honest in your evaluation of yourselves,
measuring yourselves by the faith God has
given us. ROMANS 12:3

*By being yourself,
you put something
wonderful in the world
that was not there
before.*
EDWIN ELLIOT

*Everybody is a genius.
But if you judge a fish
by its ability to climb a
tree, it will live its whole
life believing that it
is stupid.*
ALBERT EINSTEIN

*Do not wish to be
anything but what you
are, and try to be that
perfectly.*
ST. FRANCIS DE SALES

Paying for Me

God paid a ransom to save you from the empty life you inherited from your ancestors. And it was not paid with mere gold or silver, which lose their value. It was the precious blood of Christ, the sinless, spotless Lamb of God. God chose him as your ransom long before the world began, but now in these last days he has been revealed for your sake.

1 PETER 1:18-20

CONNIE HAD BIG WEEKEND PLANS! She was going to an amusement park with four of her friends. They had been planning this for weeks, and Connie was so excited! But a couple of days before the big outing, she got into a fight with her brother. They were shouting and chasing each other around the house when James pushed her and she fell . . . right into a lamp. It tumbled off the table and broke into a bazillion pieces. Of course that brought Mom running into the living room. Boy, was she mad! She immediately grounded both of them. Connie was crushed. Now she couldn't go on the trip with her friends. The more Connie begged Mom to let her go, the more firmly Mom said that she couldn't. Connie went into her bedroom and cried.

A couple of hours later, Mom came into Connie's room. "Okay, you can go to the amusement park," she said. Connie couldn't believe it. Why had Mom changed her mind? "You can thank James," Mom said. "He is taking complete blame for the fight and the broken lamp. He is willing to take all the punishment. He even asked me to let you go on the trip."

Wow. James is a pretty cool brother,

isn't he? This is a very, very small example of what Jesus has done for you. He died on the cross to take all of the punishment you deserve for the sinful things you do. Because he did that, you can be allowed into God's heaven some- day. Jesus' willingness to pay the price for your sin means you are guilt free and sin free. That's how much he loves you! Have you asked Jesus to be your Savior? Have you thanked him for his sacrifice?

CHECKUP TIME

On a scale of 1 to 5, how do you feel about Jesus' sacrifice?

1 = never
2 = not very often
3 = sometimes
4 = most of the time
5 = always

I know I can be saved because of Jesus' sacrifice.

1   2   3   4   5

I believe a price needed to be paid for my sins.

1   2   3   4   5

I think about how much Jesus loves me.

1   2   3   4   5

I thank God every day for his plan.

1   2   3   4   5

I am humbled by Jesus paying for my sins.

1   2   3   4   5

KEY

MOSTLY 1s Jesus' sacrifice is too important for you to take lightly! Ask God to make your heart more sensitive to it.

MOSTLY 2s Do you feel like this Jesus stuff is something you just think about in church? It should affect how you live every day.

MOSTLY 3s So maybe you believe in what Jesus did, but it hasn't really sunk in that it was for *you*. Pray that God will help you understand his gift!

MOSTLY 4s You believe and you've accepted Jesus' gift. Ask God to never let you take it for granted.

MOSTLY 5s Praise God! You understand the significance of what Jesus did for you.

THINGS TO DO

○ Research verses that describe your sinfulness and God's grace.

○ Read the story of Jesus' arrest and crucifixion from one of the Gospels. Read it carefully, really thinking about what it means. Try to imagine what it would have been like to be there.

○ Ask a trusted adult to explain Jesus' sacrifice to you again. Ask that person how Jesus has changed his or her life.

○ Thank God for his plan and for Jesus' sacrifice.

THINGS TO REMEMBER

Just think how much more the blood of Christ will purify our consciences from sinful deeds so that we can worship the living God. For by the power of the eternal Spirit, Christ offered himself to God as a perfect sacrifice for our sins. HEBREWS 9:14

This is how God loved the world: He gave his one and only Son, so that everyone who believes in him will not perish but have eternal life. JOHN 3:16

God showed his great love for us by sending Christ to die for us while we were still sinners. ROMANS 5:8

[The Lord] has removed our sins as far from us as the east is from the west. PSALM 103:12

When God becomes a Man and lives as a creature among His own creatures in Palestine, then indeed His life is one of supreme self-sacrifice and leads to Calvary.
C. S. LEWIS

The dying Jesus is the evidence of God's anger toward sin; but the living Jesus is the proof of God's love and forgiveness.
LORENZ EIFERT

Easter says you can put truth in a grave, but it won't stay there.
CLARENCE W. HALL

No Secrets

> O LORD, you have examined my heart and know everything about me.
>
> You know when I sit down or stand up. You know my thoughts even when I'm far away.
>
> PSALM 139:1-2

SOPHIA IS GOOD AT BEING QUIET. She thinks that she does a good job of keeping her negative and mean thoughts to herself. The honest truth is that Sophia has a lot of unkind thoughts about people. She is very critical of what others do and say as well as what they wear and how smart they are. She judges others, too, and she thinks she knows their motivations better than anyone else. Sophia believes that since she doesn't say the mean and unkind things aloud, then they don't count as sinful thoughts. She thinks that since no one knows about them then they aren't really sin.

Yeah, right. It may be true that none of Sophia's friends know what she thinks—but God does. Her thoughts are not hidden from him! Psalm 139 makes it clear that God knows our thoughts. He knows our hearts. He knows our motives. He knows everything.

How do you feel about that? Is it a good thing that God knows your thoughts and motives? Or does it mean that there are some things that you need to confess to him? He knows your secret thoughts. He knows what you say in your heart about others. You can confess and then ask his help in stopping those negative, sinful thoughts and ideas. Just remember that you have no secrets from God.

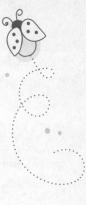

On a scale of 1 to 5, how do you feel about God knowing your thoughts?

1 = never
2 = not very often
3 = sometimes
4 = most of the time
5 = always

No big deal. I wouldn't mind telling God out loud what I'm thinking.

1 2 3 4 5

I know what I think comes out in what I say and how I act.

1 2 3 4 5

I know that what I think matters even if I don't speak my thoughts aloud.

1 2 3 4 5

I ask God to help me have positive thoughts.

1 2 3 4 5

I try to control my thoughts so that they are kind and loving.

1 2 3 4 5

KEY

MOSTLY 1s You might be fooling some people, but you're not fooling God. He cares about what's going on inside you. Ask him to help clean up your thoughts.

MOSTLY 2s You may think you're keeping all the negativity in, but sooner or later your bad thoughts will come out in your words and actions. Pray that God will help you change your thoughts before that happens.

MOSTLY 3s You know it's important to have a healthy thought life, but you're still struggling. Memorize a verse that you can say when a bad thought pops into your head.

MOSTLY 4s You know that what you think about matters. Keep replacing those negative thoughts with good ones!

MOSTLY 5s You get it! You rely on God's power to keep your thoughts about others positive.

THINGS TO DO

○ Think about a time that one of your negative thoughts eventually came out in something you said or did. Ask God to help you control your thoughts so that won't happen again.

○ Keep track of your thoughts. Are they kind? Helpful? Encouraging to others? When a negative thought pops into your mind, try praying or replacing it with a positive thought.

○ Memorize Psalm 139:1-2 so you remember that Jesus knows your thoughts.

○ Ask God to make your thoughts more like his.

THINGS TO REMEMBER

Don't copy the behavior and customs of this world, but let God transform you into a new person by changing the way you think. Then you will learn to know God's will for you, which is good and pleasing and perfect.
ROMANS 12:2

Fix your thoughts on what is true, and honorable, and right, and pure, and lovely, and admirable. Think about things that are excellent and worthy of praise. **PHILIPPIANS 4:8**

You will keep in perfect peace
all who trust in you,
all whose thoughts are fixed on you!
ISAIAH 26:3

You will experience God's peace, which exceeds anything we can understand. His peace will guard your hearts and minds as you live in Christ Jesus. **PHILIPPIANS 4:7**

Let the Spirit renew your thoughts and attitudes. Put on your new nature, created to be like God—truly righteous and holy.
EPHESIANS 4:23-24

You are today where your thoughts have brought you; you will be tomorrow where your thoughts take you.
JAMES ALLEN

Every thought is a seed. If you plant crab apples, don't count on harvesting Golden Delicious.
BILL MEYER

Our life always expresses the result of our dominant thoughts.
SØREN KIERKEGAARD

No Cheating!

If you are faithful in little things, you will be faithful in large ones. But if you are dishonest in little things, you won't be honest with greater responsibilities.

LUKE 16:10

MALIA AND JACKIE both love to play board games. Scrabble is their favorite. They love trying to stump each other with unusual words. They are both pretty good at Scrabble, but Jackie usually wins their games . . . and there's a reason for that. She cheats. Yep, she makes up words, then argues for them until Malia believes her. Jackie even convinces Malia that some words are so new to the language that they aren't even in the dictionary yet. Winning is so important to Jackie that she is willing to risk her friendship with Malia in order to win.

Why do people cheat? It's an ego thing—that feeling that the cheater *has* to be number one. Has to be first. Has to be the best. A cheater doesn't think about how her actions make other people feel. She's only thinking about what she wants.

Why is cheating so displeasing to God? His Word says that one of his most important commands is to love your neighbor. How can you love your neighbor if you are cheating her? How can you show someone that you value her if you are pushing her down by being completely self-centered and self-focused?

If you are ever tempted to cheat, remind yourself that loving others is more important than winning. Remind yourself that God commands you to love others, treat them with respect, and deal honestly with them. That's God's way. Ask God to help you treat others with respect and honesty.

CHECKUP TIME

On a scale of 1 to 5, how do you feel about cheating?

1 = never
2 = not very often
3 = sometimes
4 = most of the time
5 = always

I believe cheating is wrong.

1   2   3   4   5

I believe that winning means nothing if I have to cheat to win.

1   2   3   4   5

I know that cheating hurts my relationships.

1   2   3   4   5

When I feel tempted to cheat, I ask God to help me be honest.

1   2   3   4   5

I know that it upsets God when I cheat others, even in small things like games.

1   2   3   4   5

KEY

MOSTLY 1s You need to take a good look at your priorities. God is not impressed with your win if you have to cheat to get it. Ask him to help you be a winner in his eyes.

MOSTLY 2s Do you tell yourself it's okay to cheat every now and then on little things? God doesn't agree. Pray that he will help you resist the temptation to cheat.

MOSTLY 3s You know that cheating is wrong, but you still really love to win. Remember that you're a real winner when you decide to be honest.

MOSTLY 4s Okay, you're getting it. Cheating hurts others . . . and you. Keep playing fair!

MOSTLY 5s Great! You know that relationships are more important than winning!

THINGS TO DO

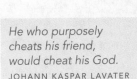

○ Think about a time when you were a victim of someone else's cheating. How did you feel? Do you want to make others feel that way?

○ Ask a friend or a parent to hold you accountable to always being honest and fair.

○ Ask God to keep you from cheating by reminding you that it's wrong.

○ Memorize Luke 16:10 so you will be reminded of the importance of honesty.

THINGS TO REMEMBER

Remember, it is sin to know what you ought to do and then not do it.
JAMES 4:17

Better to be poor and honest than to be dishonest and a fool.
PROVERBS 19:1

Do to others as you would like them to do to you. **LUKE 6:31**

A troublemaker plants seeds of strife; gossip separates the best of friends.
PROVERBS 16:28

It is better to be godly and have little than to be evil and rich. **PSALM 37:16**

He who purposely cheats his friend, would cheat his God.
JOHANN KASPAR LAVATER

He that will cheat at play, will cheat you any way.
DUTCH PROVERB

Whoever is careless with the truth in small matters cannot be trusted with important matters.
ALBERT EINSTEIN

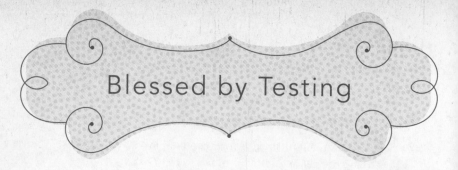

Blessed by Testing

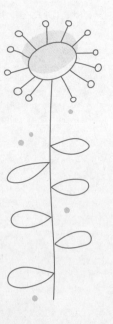

God blesses those who patiently endure testing and temptation. Afterward they will receive the crown of life that God has promised to those who love him.

JAMES 1:12

JUDY IS TIRED. Just tired. It feels like life has been one problem after another over the last few months. Her grandfather passed away, and she misses him a lot. Her aunt and uncle got a divorce, and her cousins are really sad. Judy's brother moved out, and she misses him. Her dad lost his job, and everyone is constantly worried about money. Seriously, it has been one thing after another. Judy and her family are all Christians, so they turn to God with their requests and their pain and their fears. They all believe that God hears their prayers. But Judy asks God why life has to be so painful sometimes.

That's a question you may ask God once in a while too. There isn't an easy answer, definitely not one that makes problems easier to go through. But something to remember when you seem to be drowning under constant waves of problems is that those problems keep you turning to God. Over and over and over you go to him with your requests. You go for comfort and for help. As you sense his presence with you and as you see him working on your problems, your faith in him grows stronger. So in that way you are blessed by your problems.

Is that hard to understand? Remember that the goal of your life in Christ is to grow closer to him and for your trust in him to become deeper and deeper. That doesn't happen when everything is going fine. Your trust and faith grow when you need to know God's presence and comfort. So while problems are no fun, thank God for the blessing of growing closer to him.

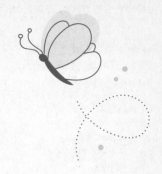

CHECKUP TIME

On a scale of 1 to 5, how do you feel about being tested?

1 = never
2 = not very often
3 = sometimes
4 = most of the time
5 = always

I believe problems are worth it if I grow closer to God.

1   2   3   4   5

Life can be tough, but I believe God is always with me.

1   2   3   4   5

With God beside me, I know I can get through any problem.

1   2   3   4   5

I learn from my problems.

1   2   3   4   5

I will stick with God no matter what happens.

1   2   3   4   5

KEY

MOSTLY 1s You're hurting right now, but shutting God out won't help. Talk to him about what you're feeling. Be honest—he can handle it.

MOSTLY 2s Do you feel deep down that if God really loved you, he'd give you an easy life? The Bible tells us about many people who were deeply loved by God and yet suffered a lot. Ask God to help you remember that he loves you no matter what you're going through.

MOSTLY 3s You know that you should be open to seeing the blessings in your problems, but sometimes it just hurts too much. Keep taking your feelings to God. Ask him to help you learn.

MOSTLY 4s You are willing to let God teach you through your problems. Keep turning to him!

MOSTLY 5s Good for you! Your faith grows stronger through what you learn during the hard times.

THINGS TO DO

- ○ Think about the last big problem you had. When it was over, what had you learned?

- ○ Memorize verses about God's help.

- ○ Ask God to help you see the lessons in times of testing.

- ○ Ask a friend or trusted adult to pray with you about your problems.

THINGS TO REMEMBER

Be strong and courageous! Do not be afraid and do not panic. . . . For the LORD your God will personally go ahead of you. He will neither fail you nor abandon you. **DEUTERONOMY 31:6**

These trials will show that your faith is genuine. It is being tested as fire tests and purifies gold—though your faith is far more precious than mere gold. So when your faith remains strong through many trials, it will bring you much praise and glory and honor on the day when Jesus Christ is revealed to the whole world. **1 PETER 1:7**

We are pressed on every side by troubles, but we are not crushed. We are perplexed, but not driven to despair. **2 CORINTHIANS 4:8**

Give your burdens to the LORD, and he will take care of you. He will not permit the godly to slip and fall. **PSALM 55:22**

Jesus said, "Come to me, all of you who are weary and carry heavy burdens, and I will give you rest." **MATTHEW 11:28**

A journey of a thousand miles begins with a single step.
CHINESE PROVERB

The difference between school and life? In school, you're taught a lesson and then given a test. In life, you're given a test that teaches you a lesson.
TOM BODETT

It is your struggles, not your successes that make you who you are. Cherish them.
MARK BLACK

The Path to Purity

How can a young person stay pure? By obeying [God's] word.
PSALM 119:9

"I WANT TO DO THE RIGHT THING, but sometimes I'm not sure what the right thing is," Emily tells her friend Cathy. "Some of my friends have this game where they go in stores and try to steal one piece of candy—nothing big. I know stealing is wrong, but this doesn't seem like such a big deal. It's just a game, after all. Those candies are hardly worth anything."

Cathy is a Christian, and she tells Emily over and over that stealing of any kind is wrong because God's Word says it is. Emily argues that no one is getting hurt. "How do I know what's right and what's wrong? Everyone has a different idea of what's right."

Cathy explains to Emily that the best way to know right and wrong is by reading and then obeying God's Word. The Bible makes pretty clear which things please God and which things do not. There are very few fuzzy lines. Stealing is definitely a "does not please God" thing.

God gave us his Word so that we can study it and learn how to live in a way that is obedient to him. Knowing God's Word and putting it in your heart and mind will help you remember it any time you have a question about whether some action is right or not.

CHECKUP TIME

On a scale of 1 to 5, how important is God's Word to you?

1 = never
2 = not very often
3 = sometimes
4 = most of the time
5 = always

God's Word? I read it every day.

1   2   3   4   5

I believe the Bible explains how to live with other people and how to obey God.

1   2   3   4   5

I want to live within God's guidelines.

1   2   3   4   5

I feel that the Bible is God's love letter to me.

1   2   3   4   5

I believe God will help me learn to love his Word.

1   2   3   4   5

KEY

MOSTLY 1s You can't live the way God wants if you treat the Bible like just another book. Ask God to give you a love for his Word.

MOSTLY 2s You know you should obey God, but it's just not that important to you right now. Pray that God will help you get your priorities straight.

MOSTLY 3s You know that the Bible is God's Word, but sometimes you struggle with obeying what it says. Ask God to help you with that.

MOSTLY 4s You are beginning to recognize the power in God's Word. Keep hiding it in your heart!

MOSTLY 5s Yay! You know that God's Word can teach you to be a better follower of Christ, and you do your best to follow its teachings.

THINGS TO DO

○ Start a plan to read through the entire Bible. It's a big job, but you don't have to rush. There are a lot of Bible-reading plans out there; find one that works for you.

○ Memorize verses about obeying God.

○ Ask God to give you a true love for his Word.

○ Ask a friend to study the Bible with you.

THINGS TO REMEMBER

I will delight in your decrees and not forget your word.
PSALM 119:16

I have hidden your word in my heart, that I might not sin against you.
PSALM 119:11

All Scripture is inspired by God and is useful to teach us what is true and to make us realize what is wrong in our lives. It corrects us when we are wrong and teaches us to do what is right. **2 TIMOTHY 3:16**

Don't just listen to God's word. You must do what it says. Otherwise, you are only fooling yourselves. **JAMES 1:22**

Your word is a lamp to guide my feet and a light for my path. **PSALM 119:105**

I've read the last page of the Bible. It's all going to turn out all right.
BILLY GRAHAM

The Bible is God's Word given in man's language.
MAX LUCADO

Within the covers of the Bible are all the answers for all the problems men face.
RONALD REAGAN

Acknowledgments

Thank you so much to Jerry Watkins, who has once again given me the opportunity to be involved in a great project to encourage young girls in their walks with Christ.

Thanks also to Sarah Rubio and the fine staff of Tyndale House Publishers. Your commitment and devotion to publishing godly products is a blessing to all who work with you.

CAROLYN LARSEN has written more than forty books for children and adults. She is best known as the author of the Little Girls Bible Storybook line of products, which have collectively sold more than one million units. In addition, Carolyn is a speaker who has taught and spoken extensively in the United States and overseas. She is the cofounder of the performing group Flashpoints, which is composed of five women who share a God-ignited passion to encourage women and girls to know God better through drama, creative movement, signing, and humor. Carolyn is the mother of three and lives with her husband in Wheaton, Illinois.

S·T·A·R·L·I·G·H·T

Animal Rescue

More than just animals need rescuing in this new series. Starlight Animal Rescue is where problem horses are trained and loved, where abandoned dogs become heroes, where stray cats become loyal companions—and where people with nowhere to fit in find a place to belong.

Entire series available now!

#1 Runaway

#2 Mad Dog

#3 Wild Cat

#4 Dark Horse

Read all four to discover how a group of teens cope with life and disappointment.

WWW.COOL2READ.COM

CP0264